LETT
OVE
THE
WALL

Life in Communist
East Germany

David F. Strack

B and L PRESS

Published by

B and L PRESS

"It's just incomprehensible that 25 years ago the prison opened, and the storm of freedom blew over us. May this storm always pull us to a spirit of insubordination and confrontation, and keep us active and never let us forget that we must constantly defend this freedom and plurality, with which we have now grown up, against ignorance and ideologues of all kinds, as we always look to the future."

- Jutta L.,
writing in 2014

Dedication

This book is dedicated to my four East German friends: Gerhard W, Jutta L, Jürgen B, and Barbara L. Without their decades of open and honest correspondence this chronicle of life in communist East Germany would not have been possible.

Acknowledgments

Without a love of travel the friendships I've written about would have never developed. And for that I thank my parents, Ray and Evie Strack. When I said, "I think I want to study abroad," there was no hesitation whatsoever in their supporting me. That meant I would be studying in Salzburg, Austria, during the spring semester of my sophomore year at the University of Redlands in 1963. And during that semester, not only spending the four months in Salzburg, but also visiting and experiencing Vienna, Rome, Prague, Paris, Munich, and London, as well as many cities and beautiful places in between, my appetite for travel was certainly whetted.

This desire to travel was also supported by the professors I had at Redlands, most importantly Dr. Henry Dittmar. With his and others' encouragement, my study of German continued, leading to a master's degree and teaching it for over forty years.

And German teachers travel to Germany. Often. And they meet people – even in the communist East.

Correspondence began with one East Berliner, and later expanded to include three other East Germans who lived in Leipzig. And what to do with nearly 100 letters, most of which were written in German? "Translate them so others can read what their lives were like," was the suggestion made by colleagues and friends. "There's a book here."

I'd like to thank friend and English teacher colleague David Braxton for reading the manuscript and making such valuable suggestions and necessary corrections.

Thanks also go to Eric Lorenzen, without whose guidance, editorial help, and knowledge of how a book gets published, I could have never completed this project.

And last, but by no means least, many thanks to my wife Bonnie for her patience and understanding during the many hours I spent translating the letters and writing the text. This whole project became at times a team effort of which she was a very important part. Thank you, Bonnie.

Table of Contents

Introduction

This all began on a beautiful sunny July 1974 afternoon in East Berlin. I was in West Berlin taking part in a seminar for thirty-three American teachers of German. We were there not only to improve our German; we also wanted to expand our knowledge of the city, its history, and its culture. And the opportunity to learn about "the other Berlin" certainly presented itself. There were five of us on that July afternoon: two from California, two from Wisconsin, and one from Texas. We had become good friends and taking a "journey" to East Berlin was something we all felt was important.

And in this city lived a very friendly East Berliner, whom we were soon to meet.

Before I get into the details of our day in East Berlin, some historical perspective is important. The victorious Allies, at the conclusion of World War II, divided Germany and its capital, Berlin, each into four zones of occupation: America, British, French, and Soviet. By 1949 two Germanys were in existence: West Germany, officially called the Federal Republic of Germany (FRG), and East Germany, the German Democratic Republic (GDR). The Federal Republic was established out of the

American, British and French zones and its capital was Bonn, on the Rhine River, not far from Cologne; the Democratic Republic was the Soviet zone, its capital being the Soviet-controlled part of Berlin, the eastern section of the city. West Berlin - the combined American, French, and British zones – then became, in effect, an "island in a sea of communism."

On August 13, 1961, the Soviet-backed East German regime forcefully stopped its citizens from going to the western part of the city; millions of East Germans had been fleeing to the Federal Republic through West Berlin. This date marks the beginning of the building of the Berlin Wall. The East German government said an "anti-fascist protective barrier" had to be erected for national security reasons. This wall eventually surrounded all of West Berlin, even preventing East German citizens who did not live in East Berlin from entering the American, British and French zones.

Going into East Berlin for Americans was an interesting, if not at times, intimidating experience: There was the passport check at Checkpoint Charlie by friendly U.S. Army personnel; one then walked through an area which many Westerners called "no man's land" – an area about 50 meters wide between the two checkpoints; finally a second passport check by East Berlin border guards concluded the experience. I'll never forget their cold, somewhat unfriendly demeanor when they compared my passport picture with my face.

The process continued with a thorough search of whatever backpack or bag I carried, followed by questions about the purpose of the visit or whom I might be visiting. And finally, admittance and the stamping of my passport with a visa that was good until midnight of that day.

One also had to pay the *Zwangsumtausch*, the "forced exchange" of a minimum of 25 West marks for 25 East marks. But this was not a good deal. A West mark was worth five East marks, when exchanged officially in West Berlin. So exchanging 25 West marks would have amounted to 125 East marks if done in West Germany. But the East German government did not allow the importation of any of its East Mark currency from the Federal Republic, so there was no choice but to "purchase" the East marks, which amounted to only 25 marks, instead of 125 marks. This was all accomplished when entering East Berlin.

This one-to-one exchange became very "profitable" for the government of the German Democratic Republic; it was a major source of West marks, which had to be used when purchasing goods and materials from West Germany.

My first experience in East Berlin took place in the summer of 1966. The Wall at that time stood about eight feet high with barbed wire strung along its entire upper surface. But by the mid-1970s it was over twelve feet high, and virtually impossible to scale or climb over.

Now, back to that July day in 1974. Exchange we did, and in

we went. It reminded us of paying the entrance fee to an amusement park. East Berlin, however, had no similarity to an amusement park; it was a drab and gray city, with Stalin-era apartment blocks and limited shopping opportunities.

Occasionally we would even see Soviet soldiers.

There were also, compared to West Berlin, very few automobiles. The vast majority of the traffic consisted of Trabants – or "Trabis" – the "people's car." They were powered by three-cylinder, two-stroke engines that spewed clouds of blue oil smoke whenever they started moving.

However, East Berlin was also a city rich in history, with many pre-war buildings restored to their original beauty, a magnificent cathedral, broad boulevards, and a radio and television tower over one thousand feet high.

The five of us become good friends and this "trip" to East Berlin was something we all felt was important. So – after checking in – off we went. Walking. And walking. Not really knowing where we were going. But that didn't matter. We knew we were in East Berlin, and we wanted to experience what we could of the city.

It wasn't long before hunger set in, and it was time for lunch. But where to eat? A quick hamburger at McDonald's? Not possible. We soon found ourselves in an area of the city that didn't appear to have any restaurants. There was, however, a small city park with a man sitting on a bench. After exchanging greetings and telling him where we were from, he informed us we were the first Americans he'd ever met. Gerhard was his name, and he was relaxing, having just gotten off work.

But we were still hungry, and when we asked about a restaurant, he was more than happy to direct us to one not too far away. After a short walk, we found the restaurant: It was very nice with white tablecloths, silverware, and waiters dressed in what amounted to tuxedos. So non-East Berlinisch, actually. And not really very expensive. But way too fancy for us and what we wanted to eat. We wanted a place where normal, working-class people would eat.

So we continued walking. Within about 30 minutes, Gerhard rode up on his motor scooter, having changed out of his work clothes. "You didn't like the place?" he asked. "Beautiful, but too nice for us," was our reply. We really wanted a *gut bürgerliches Restaurant*, a place where common folk would eat. That was our request, and that's where all of us – including Gerhard - wound up. Soon we were eating roast pork, mashed potatoes and veggies, and drinking lots of beer. Total cost: about 2$ US per person, even at the forced exchange rate. And the afternoon then became an evening at Gerhard's very modest two-room flat with more beer. And Russian vodka chasers.

11:30 pm came very quickly. "Visa time" was about to expire. It was just before midnight, and after a cab ride back to the East Berlin border crossing opposite Checkpoint Charlie, that we ever so slowly walked back across "no-man's land" to West Berlin. We were out, but we had a new friend.

In August the language institute ended. But not before we were able to visit Gerhard a few more times. Friendships developed – but it was time to return home. In 1975 a correspondence began that still exists through emails today in 2015.

Little did I know then that three more East Germans would be added to the "East German friends' list." In the summer of 1983, Ivan Schreiber – my close friend from La Jolla, California, who was also in our 1974 group – and I attended a German teachers' seminar at the University of Leipzig, Leipzig being a very important city in East Germany. Here we met Jürgen, Jutta, and Barbara. They were university students and assistants in our seminar groups.

So – now I knew four East Germans with whom I could correspond.

Thirty-six years after that summer of 1975 – in 2011 - I came across a box of letters on a shelf in a closet. Not really forgotten, but not looked at in years. More than 80 letters from East Germany, all in German, except for Jutta's, which are in English. I asked myself: "How will my kids be able to read the ones in German when they find this box of letters?"

I started translating the letters into English and quickly realized there's a very interesting chronicle of the lives of four

East Germans over a period of nearly forty years. Important years for the German Democratic Republic: The mid-1970s, up through the mid-1980s, which were intense years of the Cold War; Reagan, Gorbachev, *glasnost, perestroika* and the eventual relaxation of some travel restrictions for East Germans in the late 80s; the "revolution" and fall of the Wall on November 9, 1989. These are events that led to great changes in the lives of the people of East Germany. Most of them good, some not so good.

These letters – while only windows into the lives of four individuals - give a certain insight into what life was like in the GDR during those years. And this might be of value to those who are interested in "things German" and life in East Germany during and after the Cold War. What follows are excerpts from the letters which can help the reader understand aspects of "East German life" during these years. I should also note that in order to protect my friends' privacy, I'm not using their real names: Gerhard, Jürgen, Barbara and Jutta are pseudonyms.

I'm approaching this in four major chronological sections:

1) Insights into and descriptions of my friends' lives in East Germany from the mid-1970s to the late 1980s. What were the challenges? What were the frustrations? What made life difficult? What made life pleasant?

2) How these individuals perceived and reacted to the great changes about to take place in November of 1989.

3) The 1990s: The Wall is gone. Germany is united again.

What changed? Were these changes for the better? What difficulties were faced and how did lives change in the years immediately after unification.

4) The second decade of the twenty-first century: After a rather long pause, our correspondence still takes place through email. One of them is retired and the other three continue leading busy and successful lives.

My wife, Bonnie, and I were able to see all our East German friends in November 2014; we were in Berlin for the celebrations commemorating the 25th anniversary of the opening of the Wall. I'll conclude this chronicle by describing our time together during those very special days and by updating the reader on how Gerhard, Jutta, Barbara and Jürgen are doing in 2015.

CHAPTER ONE

1975

As I mentioned earlier, a group of us met Gerhard on that sunny July afternoon in East Berlin in 1974. He was 31 years old; the same age as I was. (Our birthdays are three days apart, his being September 14, mine being September 11.)

His first letter to me is dated January 7, 1975:

Thank you so very much for your nice letter and the pictures. You can't imagine how happy it makes me to get a letter from America… Here I am in East Germany seemingly cut off from everything that one would call "internationalism." It's especially great for me to have friends in the "enemy country," which is not looked upon here so positively, but also which one can't keep me from doing.

Contact with us was not forbidden, and he's also able to learn about the USA:

I can see lots of films here about America, but I can't really relate to them because everything is so foreign to me. When I see pictures of places where friends live, I can then create for myself a relationship to those friends. I can look at your pictures for hours and imagine how it would be to be there. This gets me "high" for a long time. Until now I'd had no contact with Americans and always observed them with mixed feelings. But now I know what a beloved and romantic people they can be. For us here work is always the most important thing, and if one doesn't develop a lot of personal initiative for free time activities, life becomes really boring.

Travel is something that Gerhard always wanted to do. A key destination was the Soviet Union. But:

> I wanted this coming summer to take a trip to the Soviet Union – our "best friend." One is only allowed to do that on prescribed and approved routes. But I didn't get permission because politically I'm just not so dedicated to communism.

Romania would be a nice second choice: "Fine, I'll just try Romania – if I get permission." He concludes these travel comments with:

> So – that's how it goes here with freedom. Don't ever believe I'd come back here if I some day should be allowed to visit you in California. That would probably take a hundred years – especially since I'm not allowed to even go to the Soviet Union. But let's leave this sad topic. I can only regret that that's the way it is.

He thanked us for various items we'd sent him: 1) two ceramic tequila glasses from Ivan, 2) a belt buckle stamped with the word "Texas" from Bob, and 3) a calendar with many pictures from Marilyn's hometown in Wisconsin.

> I'm really happy to get packages but, to be honest, letters and pictures make me even happier. Those I can't buy – contents of packages I can. Speaking of buying: with the dollars and marks you guys sent me I was able to shop in a special store for jeans and cosmetics. Those are things the quality and quantity of which I just can't get here for East German marks. . . . I can't buy a flat: I can only take what the government offers on contract. The new apartment would be just as bad as

my old one. Didn't it shock you, how I live compared to how you live? I don't go hungry, no, but my earnings just don't allow me any extra to eat.

Gerhard concludes this first letter with comments which show, to me at least, how sensitive a person he is:

I still just can't understand that you guys liked it so much here. As proof of this I took your silence after you all got home. I thought a lot about why no one wrote. Did I behave badly, or do I live so poorly or was your departure just too restrained for Americans? I meant everything with complete honesty, and I cried when you all left at the border, because with your departure I felt I had practically lost you all. I really thought such improbable and good friends had said farewell forever.

And then nothing came in the mail and I had to assume you had forgotten me or didn't have pleasant thoughts of your visit with me. Now I'm a little sad because you are all so far away. But now I have your addresses and as soon as someone writes me, I'll write back...

David F. Strack

CHAPTER TWO

1977

And write back he did. I learned more about life in the GDR: "A lot is still forbidden here – naturally that I have contact with my 'enemies.' But that just makes me want to have more contact with them . . . I need contact with normal people."

In this first letter of 1977 he wrote about his service in the East German army:

I would never have believed that the state would spend so much money on something so stupid. You'd never imagine what a bunch of jerks our army is. Everything is falling apart... and all the officers can talk about is just a bunch of crap. It just appears to me that all of those who are too lazy to do honest work just go into the army and become officers.

If there ever is a war and the Americans come we'd have only one chance: The Americans would laugh when they see us. I don't believe we'd be an opponent that anyone would take seriously.

With all the uselessness that goes on here I naturally have some advantages: I really don't have to sweat much. In order to have some peace and quiet, all I have to do at target practice is to always hit the target – and to my surprise, I'm successful. It's almost fun to be on maneuvers and to have to sleep in the woods. Don't think that I'm a good soldier.

My boss is an especially stupid major. I'll soon be out of the army, and then I can begin to live a normal life.

Gerhard wrote extensively about how much he appreciated our writing to him, the gifts we had sent, and what he'd learned about the USA. He also described his living conditions:

> I live in a flat in a very old building. We have only one room, the kitchen and a hallway. It's eventually getting better because many new buildings are being built now and they are also very cheap. But they are all buildings for lots of people. No one has a yard. But we're happy, mainly because we don't really know anything any better. And besides, we couldn't really afford a house with a yard.

His vacation activities and travel during these years were limited; motorcycle rides and camping in the mountains of East Germany were about all he could do outside of East Berlin. His comments about this city give good insight into what life was like in the capital of the Democratic Republic during the 1970s:

> We live here in a strange country and in an even stranger city. Especially here in the city, the division between East and West is just crazy. Railroad, streetcar lines and streets end suddenly at the border, many houses are even divided. When I stand at the border and look at the people and buildings on the other side - it's a very strange feeling. And they are Germans - even my relatives - and I'm not allowed to visit them. If I were to illegally go over the border I would be shot or would spend two years in prison. I'm not allowed at all to travel to a capitalistic country; therefore I can never visit you. In West Germany the people live better, and if the border were open, many people would leave this country and want to live there.

In the GDR, workers are needed, and if all of them left, who would then do the work?

He continues with this short description of his job: "I work as an assembler for an automatic drilling machine in a company that makes carburetors. My work is very interesting and I'm paid very well... I earn 1200 Marks per month."

He also writes that his 250cc motorcycle had cost 3500 Marks. That was nearly three months wages.

He concludes this letter with a description of German Christmas traditions – Saint Nicolas' arrival in early December, the wonderful music that's played, his parents decorating the tree on Christmas Eve, and the discovering it on Christmas morning with the gifts brought by the Christ Child. "I was a fresh little kid who just loved Christmas."

But times have changed:

Right after the war we were very poor, and my most prized possessions were a flashlight or a bicycle. Today kids look forward to motorcycles or tape players.

But eventually we became pretty rich and things were going very well.

David F. Strack

Early Photos of the Wall

Author's first view of the Wall. (1966)

Another view of the Wall in 1966

Checkpoint Charlie in the earlier years.

Viewing platform from the West (East Germans blocked the view with large sign promoting friendship and peace)

Streets were severed by the Wall.

"The Soviet Union was, is, and will remain the best friend of the German people."

Original Wall was built so quickly that it was often crooked.

Barbed wire on the Wall

CHAPTER THREE

1982

Our correspondence picked up considerably in the 1980s. In 1982 Gerhard wrote that he had a typewriter. He apologizes in advance for "missing letters and misspellings" in his typing. But I'll probably be getting more mail from him. He has a new hobby:

> I've been taking pictures for some time now for slides. . . .
> Naturally I'll send you some typical scenes from here that
> might be very interesting to your students, something first
> hand to experience communism.

He concludes this letter describing how one obtained a car in the GDR:

> This coming March I could buy a car, if I had the money. Ten
> years ago I put my name in, and now I've learned that I can
> buy a Mazda 323. But it costs 25,000 Marks, which I just don't
> have.
>
> The motorcycle will have to suffice.

In May of 1982 he wrote that pictures I said I had sent were not in my latest letter. I couldn't remember if I'd ever sent them.

Look on your desk and you'll discover them. I don't think someone took them out because no one's ever done that. Now I'm really looking forward to your next letter because there will certainly be more pictures in it.

He also commented about young people in the GDR and in the USA.

I'm amazed at the many and beautiful interests your children have. I've got to believe that it's completely normal that their parents foster kids' talents and abilities. Here that's not the norm and most kids just bore themselves on the streets and have only very unhealthy hobbies. They smoke and drink and [the boys] only think of girls. On the beaches and in the parks they are very loud and leave a big mess. I've certainly done all that, too. I just think that the kids in California are different, or am I wrong?

I don't think he was completely wrong.

I had planned a tour of Germany with a group of my high school students for the summer of 1982, and Berlin was on the itinerary. He expressed how much he was looking forward to meeting them:

Please bring as many kids and others as you can. There won't be any problems here at my place. It's too bad that it will be so short. Perhaps they'd like to have a discussion with some of my friends. What would they all like to drink? At any rate, it's going to be great – that I can tell already.

We were able to meet and it was a memorable afternoon –

especially for my students. In addition to being in East Berlin and seeing the highlights of the city, they enjoyed meeting Gerhard, being in his apartment, and learning a bit about how an East German lived.

In this letter he also made some interesting comments about communicating by telephone in the GDR:

> Two of my neighbors have phones. But they're often in their garden in the summer. So here's the number of my other neighbor. But he's with the police and it's best if you don't tell him where you're calling from.

The summer of 1982 was also a time of travel for Gerhard. He was able to go to Poland in 1981 for "relaxed and undisturbed weekends," but in 1982 that wasn't going to happen: "They [the government] won't let me and other Germans do that. They're just so afraid here of the idea of free trade unions that all contact is being suppressed." (The Solidarity movement, led by Lech Walesa, was causing considerable unrest in Poland at that time.) He then writes he'll probably spend his vacation in Czechoslovakia. Some interesting comments on further travel restrictions then follow; he would like to ride his motorcycle to the Soviet Union, but he's not allowed to.

> Why, I don't know. One can do it by car. But you still have to follow a specific travel route and stay exactly on schedule. The roads are strictly monitored and they call ahead like you're a train in route. And if you don't get to the next checkpoint on

time you're stopped, searched and fined. Personal contact is also not allowed and also impossible.

We always read here in the newspaper: The Soviets are our brothers. But we say in jest: "One can choose one's friends, but not one's brothers."

Gerhard, however, isn't completely critical life in the GDR. Some things seem to be fine:

In contrast to all the countries around us there's nothing new in East Germany. Prices are, to my great astonishment, the same and otherwise all else is peaceful and solid. It's astonishing that gasoline prices have been the same since 1945. We really have all we need. For my flat I could buy new furniture, and I also have a beautiful stronger radio and a new TV. But I still don't have enough for a car. I just got my driver's license just in case I come across a cheap car.

The visit with the students to East Berlin took place in June of 1982. How that went is summed up in the first paragraph of Gerhard's letter dated June 23rd:

I'm writing to you today so the impressions of the day are fresh in my mind because you'll certainly be home a while before it gets to your mailbox. It's too bad we were together today for such a short time that there really wasn't a good opportunity to get a proper mood going with your students. It wasn't until you all disappeared through that ugly door that it hit me that I might never see you again – or at least not for a very long time. Your departure was so extraordinarily sincere that it really got to me. I had assumed that the time here was not very enjoyable at all. I also thought that they had expected more from their 25 Mark entrance fee into the communist world. But this surprisingly emotional departure made me really happy. I would like to thank you all for your tact and your interest.

He continues by describing how much he likes and appreciates American music, asking what we all did in West Germany, and what he could send me – magazines and newspaper, or slides – that would be interesting to my students. This offer comes "because you aren't able to buy everything from East Germany there." Gerhard is truly hoping that a long and lasting relationship develops.

It did.

This letter concludes with his plans for the summer:

My vacation starts in two weeks and, as usual, I'll just ride around the countryside on my motorcycle. But not just riding around because I still want to go to Czechoslovakia. It's really pretty cheap there, the people are friendly, and the countryside, with its beautiful mountains, is such a wonderful change. Besides I feel better there than at home. When I stay in East Germany all the signs that tell me what I can't do make me angry. In a Czech camping site one can do pretty much what one wants to do. For example, here campfires are forbidden everywhere. There not. And camping without a campfire is unthinkable, right?

Gerhard writes he'd already received a letter from one of my students who, he says, seemed "to be extremely interested and there just wasn't the time to answer any questions."

In November he wrote back to this student and she passed the letter on to me. He begins: "You don't need to worry about me– weeds and bad people are always doing well." He apologizes for not writing sooner because he had been so busy with summer activities:

> And that is to ride all around on my motorcycle with my tent. That's how I spend my vacation and how I meet friends and people who think like me. Naturally I like it in a foreign country the best. But sadly my opportunities are really limited. And there's really only one country that I can go to, as I want. After the borders to Poland were closed I can only go to Czechoslovakia without having to go to the police first. For all other countries I must get permission. But it's just beautiful being with the Czechs – they have such beautiful mountains and good beer.

He continues by responding to the questions that my student had asked in a letter she had written to him:

> You wanted to know something about East Germany? Things really aren't so bad, and many people are content.

> But there are areas where one can't get West German TV. I think there are more communists in those areas than here in Berlin because people there can't see how the rest of the world looks. Our TV is just really boring and full of Russian movies. There's nothing more boring: The communist hero can never be defeated. A normal person just can't watch this stuff.

But American films seem to be fine: "When an American film plays here the place is full. When a Russian film is playing nobody goes. Sometimes school kids are forced to watch these Russian films."

Gerhard's comments on Russian soldiers were also very enlightening:

> There is just no sympathy here at all for the Russians. The normal Russian soldier isn't allowed to even take a walk without being accompanied by an officer, they aren't allowed to go to restaurants and nobody has contact with them. I feel sorry for them because it's like a prison in their barracks. That's because they'll just get drunk and then no woman will be safe. Every day I read in the newspaper that the Russians are our best friends. I don't know any personally...

This letter concludes with an interesting comment on the communist system:

> Theory and practice are also very different things in communism. Only about 3 million of our 17 million people are registered communists. And many of them are only in the Communist Party because it advances their career. Anybody in a managerial position must be in the Party. Otherwise he won't be a manager. You see, then, I can never advance because I'm not a communist.

In 1982 Gerhard also wrote to my friend Ivan, who was one of our group in Berlin. Ivan passed on to me a copy of a letter in which Gerhard describes some interesting aspects of his life:

- He loves watching the TV show Dallas: "J.R. was finally shot."

- Music: country/western is his favorite.

- Transportation: the motorcycle needs repair; he still doesn't have enough money for a car, even though he's working on getting his driver's license. But he prefers his motorcycle to driving a car:

To be honest: The motorcycle is more fun. When I get out of the car I'm just pooped. That's because a car is so suffocating. I just need to have the wind in my face. . . . There's a new bike with 21 horsepower. I just might buy it. I could go 140km/hour [87 mph] with no problem. But I really shouldn't drive so fast because the speed limit is 100km/hour [62 mph] – but it's just a beautiful feeling to have a little extra power in reserve. My dream is to get a big Honda…

But things were actually improving, in Gerhard's opinion, for the people of the GDR:

All in all, I'm doing fine and others are gradually, too. In contrast to neighboring countries, things here aren't getting more expensive, and not as much is missing in the stores as before. For example, it surprises me that the cost of gasoline has been constant since 1945.

And since the GDR has just purchased an entire American company we can now get really good jeans. At 150 Marks they're a bit expensive, but we're happy to be able to buy them.

Cassette players, are, however, quite expensive: A Cr02 type costs 45 Marks. It's really annoying and I just don't understand how those responsible can let such things happen.

Competition with the West is also mentioned in this letter:

We've still got quite a bit to go before we overtake the West. I'll probably never experience it. If I believe what is in the newspaper, we live in a paradise. Who knows if they've got such prices in the West? But for my apartment I pay only about 60 Marks a month. That's the other side, and what I can save through cheap housing costs means I can pay over inflated prices for other things.

Interestingly, Gerhard writes that he spends considerable time at the U.S embassy in East Berlin:

> I still have good contact with the American embassy and I'm there at my regular hour in the library. I just love the fantastic pictures of the USA; the librarian helps me a lot.
>
> When I'm there I really feel I'm in another world. I can say what I want and read what would otherwise be forbidden. But there could be problems when I leave the building because the police are always there, and I'm told they will check me to see if I've got any forbidden reading materials. I was checked once, but not since then because I'm registered, and they saw that I had good reason to visit the embassy. Now they leave me alone.

He doesn't elaborate on what his "good reason" is. He concludes this letter by being quite critical of young East Berliners:

> It's too bad that many young people who lean toward committing crimes go to the library and steal books. The staff there just has so much trust: one only has to give name and address. It's too bad a few pigs shamelessly misuse this trust. I'm ashamed.

In August of 1982 Gerhard writes again about travel. I'd written to him about how much my students enjoyed their visit to East Berlin, how worthwhile our visit was, and how important it had been for me personally to learn more about East Germany.

> I still can't believe that your visit with me meant so much to all of you. Naturally I'm very happy about that; I just thought that East Berlin was just one station out of many. But now I know better, and in the future I can focus more on it. My being able to visit California? Not going to happen: A trip to California would be for me simply unbelievable. But the fact is, I'll never get there, out of Europe, into another system.

As we'll see, that all changed in 1989. He concludes:

> I don't think I have the correct image of Americans: They don't appear to be as spoiled as I thought. The fact that I'm awaiting more mail, and thereby have new friends, makes me especially happy. Please tell them that it's no problem if they write in English. I'll have no problem reading it. It would be best if they would type the letters, though.

He also asked that we send him stuff. (I can't really use a better word.)

> T-shirts showing anything from the USA, and slides of anything that will bring me closer to your homeland. It's too bad I can't get any posters of motorcycles. Linda sent me some once, but I didn't get them because here they are forbidden because they are advertising materials. Maybe when you come next time you could wrap a poster around your waist.

Didn't happen. Too much contact with "evil capitalists" was forbidden.

CHAPTER FOUR

1983

In 1983 my friend Ivan and I were accepted to the summer program at the University of Leipzig for teachers of German. This led to contact with three more East Germans. After a brief stopover in East Berlin and further contact with Gerhard, we soon found ourselves at the university in the "City of Bach."

Leipzig is a city rich in music and history.

It is the home of the Thomas Church, where Johann Sebastian Bach spent several decades as director of music. The Gewandhaus, with its world-renowned orchestra, is also located here.

And the Nikolai Church is in Leipzig. This is where, in 1989, the demonstrations that eventually led to the fall of the East German regime, began.

But we were there to improve our German and to experience another city of the German Democratic Republic, not to take part in any revolution.

Our time here led to three new friendships. And, as with Gerhard, we have corresponded for years on quite a regular basis.

Let me briefly introduce them:

Jürgen was the graduate assistant in my language group. He was a very intelligent and out-going young man of twenty years old working toward a degree in Germanic studies. He very ably assisted the professor of our group in our daily class sessions.

Jutta, now mother of a young daughter, held the same position in Ivan's seminar. She was pursuing a degree in Germanic studies and English translation. It was soon very obvious that she wanted to get to know Americans better, and this led to her inviting us to dinner in her apartment. It turned out to be a most memorable evening, as I will describe later.

Barbara greeted Ivan and me in Leipzig's main train station. She had been assigned to meet us as we stepped off the train. We were surprised as she greeted us; I guess we just looked like Americans. She was very nice, very friendly, and very helpful. And very pretty. She escorted us to the registration center not far from the station.

(My correspondence with Barbara was facilitated by Jürgen, but it didn't begin until 1986.)

As we spent our weeks in Leipzig we got to know these three quite well. Friendships developed, and the letters we exchanged give even more insight and understanding into the lives of East German citizens during a period of tremendous change.

My correspondence with the "Leipzigers" began in the fall of 1983, after my return to the USA.

It took a while in the 80s for letters to reach their destination.

Jutta, who always wrote in English, let me know that she got my letter of September 27th in the middle of November. "That's life... You see, I'm no lazy type who doesn't answer letters. I'm really crazy about writing letters. Nowadays an admirable feature, isn't it?" Yes – and it was so much appreciated.

> It's interesting to read about the echo to your journey to the GDR from your friends' part. It was nice to read that I somehow was contributing to international understanding: So one can say that you contributed to mankind's awareness that somewhere on earth is a small spot called the GDR, which is distinguished from Germany.

As we shall see, Jutta is a very sensitive, intelligent and worldly-wise person, always reaching out beyond the borders of her country.

Here she inferred that there were travel restrictions, apparently having been denied permission to visit friends. She apparently had made up a story of an accident which was her excuse for not being able to attend class at the University. Her comment to me was: "As to my accident with the ladder, I can admit that it was just pretended. I left Leipzig with my daughter in order to visit friends. *Top secret!!*"

A happy face follows her "top secret" remark.

Jutta then comments on her goals in life, writing:

> We have the same intentions and ambitions so that we'll make the very best of our lives. Who knows how long this earth will

remain safe. So my hedonistic feelings sometimes climb to chaotic heights. I like to gather all friends around a great fireplace to sing and drink like the German expressionists did in the midst of World War I, thinking that possibly the end of the world was coming.

Nevertheless, I hope that behind our anxiety and fear will be a future. I hope it for our children!

As things turned out, there definitely was a future for Jutta and her children. She believed in this future in 1983. I wrote the following in my journal on July 21, 1983, describing that dinner evening in her apartment:

Ivan and I then went to Jutta's place. Her friend Jörg was there. It was a very pleasant candle-lit evening with interesting conversation. They maintain things are very tight. Luther year, the 500th anniversary celebrations of his birth, is just a showcase. She vows she'll get to California. As she said that, the Beatles' song *Let It Be* began playing on her stereo. Unbelievable.

Little did we know then that her being in California would "be" in 1998. More on that later.

CHAPTER FIVE

1984

Gerhard writes in January about the Cold War: "As I'm taught, Americans are very poorly informed about world politics and most don't have any interest."

He continues by telling me about the availability of Western television and Radio Free Berlin. They were both readily available in East Berlin during these years. He has some rather strong opinions about the perils of the Cold War: "As you know, it's possible for me to get informed from both sides through TV and radio. Therefore, I've got my own opinions about the Pershing missiles and SS 20s." These were the key missiles both sides were deploying in the 1980s. His opinion as to why these missiles – which if ever used in Europe would completely destroy so many countries – were developed, is as follows:

> There have been Russian rockets for 15 years already, they were called SS 5 then, but were of about the same quality as the SS 20. The Pershing [the missile developed in the USA to counter the SS-20s] needed, from concept to final readiness about 12 years. During all those years nobody was talking about Russian superiority. Not until the Pershing was developed and ready to bring on line did anyone speak of

equality and equity. With this trick the American military establishment wanted to convince the taxpayers of the ridiculous expenditures.

The Americans create an impossible fuss in Geneva and know from the beginning that the negotiations are only being carried out so that stupid normal citizens don't protest too much and above all serve to get Reagan re-elected. Finally it's the Russians' fault. Bullshit.

Reagan is finally just a straw puppet that only does what is demanded by big industry. And now he must sell the rockets and needs an alibi to do it. The dumb ones are those who do the work and get no profits from industry.

* * *

Jutta also writes about her fear of the arms' race. She was and is a very skilled translator of English texts into German. This was not a translation assignment, but she writes in this letter about something she had read in English: It was about "having to work over a manual of military medicine called 'The Mass Catastrophe' and deals with mass disasters 'in peace and war.' The latter one is the atomic disaster."

She then uses rather graphic English:

I could vomit in the way they treat that theme as a sports event, through which one can test one's abilities of organizing and managing the treatment of thousands or millions of atomically "injured" people...Shit.

* * *

Gerhard also continues to express his opinions about the

worldwide dangers of the missile industry:

> I believe you must also suffer under this. Why would one want to be rather dead than socialist or capitalist? People can live under both systems. If there were no weapons we'd all be OK.

> I'd really fight against a system like Hitler's, but that doesn't exist anymore. What is one really afraid of? Are Americans afraid of socialism? I, anyway, would be happy if we had a capitalistic system. One only has one life and one must make the most of it. But when I compare how you live and how we live, you've got to understand what I mean.

He worked hard. Things that many Americans take for granted and were quite affordable in the West, were not easily purchased in the GDR.

> Yesterday I bought a pair of shoes for 144 Marks. My color TV cost 4100 Marks. The average monthly salary for an East German worker is 1,130 marks per month.

> How can I be happy with my life when I work my whole life long only for my flat and clothing and finally I'm still just a poor man? But I need to put this in perspective: Surely we have it better than all the other socialist countries, but we also work harder than they. . . . Everything we do has to be directed at the Soviet Union.

He followed this comment with a joke that must have been popular at that time. A guy says: "In the Ukraine the wheat stalks are like telephone poles." "What?" his friend asks. "They're that high?" "No, just that far apart."

He concludes with this statistic: "The industrial output of the socialist countries, in my opinion, stands at 1/20th of that of the capitalist countries. Naturally, I mean the industrialized countries."

With this letter Gerhard also includes headlines from East Berlin newspapers, which I found interesting:

- "Hundreds of thousands of American workers are shifted around like slaves"
- "Reaching into the pockets of the common people"
- "More than half of all students fail their English exam"

[The article referred to tests given in the state of Maryland.]

- "Pershing 2 Rockets were never a means to catch up"

And he has a sense of humor, as evidenced in his concluding sentences:

Hopefully, someday we'll have time to discuss this, if you're interested. But don't think I'm going to get gray hair because of all of this. I'll make the best of it, and there are women everywhere. Isn't that most important? A little love and tenderness and everything is forgotten, yes, even if at any moment an SS 20 or Pershing missile can fall on one's head. So – head up, old boy, and don't let all of this beat us down.

* * *

In her letter in February Jutta writes, in English, that she was surprised to learn my wife and I had three children, thinking we'd had just one. Her comments on family size:

It's very comforting to me to find people who have more than two children. That's a sign of being largely unaffected by attitudes, which are typical for consumerist societies. (Do you know that the population of West Germany is likely to be diminished by 50% (!!) by the year 2000, as people don't like to miss any convenience?

Obviously that decrease did not happen. I have no idea from where she got that information. And in East Germany? She wrote, "The tendency for having fewer and fewer children is also to be seen in the GDR."

She concludes by saying that she would like to have one or two more children.

And she did have two more. She was finally able to get to California in 1998 and visited us with her two sons, ages ten and twelve. She was raising them to experience the world in a way she never could as a child. A highpoint of their stay was a road trip from Southern California through parts of Arizona, stopping in Las Vegas on the way to San Francisco. On the day they were to leave she brought me a road map and asked: "What's the best way to get to Death Valley from Las Vegas." It was mid-August. My reply: "Jutta – it's August and it's really too hot to visit Death Valley now." "Oh – that's ok," she replied. "I want the boys to experience 50 degrees Celsius." (That's 122 degrees Fahrenheit.)

They drove through Death Valley.

And her children love to travel.

Back to 1984: In her February letter, we learn something more of Jutta's appreciation for nature and her surroundings:

Looking from my desk out of the window I can see snowflakes dancing weightlessly in the air. This causes me tranquility and other good feelings. From time to time a train passes by, and the streetcar creaks when slowly taking the curve of the final station. I like this; I'm a typical *Stadtmensch*. [A person who loves living in a city.]

And life experiences for her two-year-old daughter are now beginning: "Tomorrow Julia will go to the theatre for the very first time in her life. We'll see Cinderella. I can't wait! She is very smart and clever and already knows a whole lot of fairy-tales."

* * *

An interesting exchange of letters developed between Jürgen and me in 1984. We had sent each other articles from the print media in our respective countries. He comments on this in a letter written in April, apologizing for not having any "true commentary at hand" to what I had sent him. "We just don't have a large selection of newspapers here. And others aren't available in the kiosks."

He then writes about the Cold War arms' race:

Also interesting are the lists - found in an article you sent me - in which the initiatives in the USSR that deal with the stationing of rockets there are described. I don't think this is so well known in the USA.

And I'm sending you the latest article from this morning's *Leipiziger Zeitung*, which contains an interview with Mikhail

Gorbachev dealing with strategic arms limitations. Is it known in the USA that until November of 1985 the Soviets will station no more rockets? What do you think? How will the USA react?

In this context the articles you sent me also need to be looked at. Unfortunately, I don't have them here so I can't write any more about them now. The texts are in the university – my English teacher is using them in her seminars. The US representatives certainly have high hopes for these negotiations. But let's wait until the first signs of progress – or non-progress – are evident. The Soviets are certainly going forward by setting a good example.

One of the articles I sent Jürgen dealt with the Semper Opera in Dresden, one of Europe's finest opera venues. His reaction:

The article about the Semper Opera was excellent. It addresses a topic, which we've often discussed: the exchange of people, in this case artists, in order to enrich cultural life. I can identify with the author – it's exactly how I feel.

In this same letter he writes about a recently taken oral English exam. He had to talk about another article that I had sent him, although now I can't recall what that topic was. His comment gives us some more insight into "cultural life" in the GDR, which seemed to be quite restricted:

Two weeks ago I had my English exam. In it I talked about the article you sent me, and we (English teacher, assessor, and I) had the same opinion. So - we are also critical! But it's good to hear an opinion from another continent. When that doesn't happen, one can kind of get stuck in a middle ground. Therefore I'd really be excited if sometime a singer or designer from the USA could enrich our cultural life.

But such a thing just won't happen within our borders. For example, here in our theater in almost every production certain "stars" always play the lead roles. We could really use some variation here.

An anti-war postcard that was very popular in the GDR during these years accompanied this letter. It shows a ruined cityscape, obviously after war had taken place. The caption under the picture reads: *"War ist die Vergangenheitsform von sein."* ["War is the past tense form of to be."] There's a very clever play on words here: *Sein* is the German infinitive of the verb "to be." The past tense form of this verb in German is *war*, which means "was" in English – which just happens to be spelled the same as a well-known English noun: "war."

A prominent recurring theme in the GDR during the mid-80s was calling for an end to nuclear weapons. Jürgen includes with this letter a newspaper article wherein an interview of Mikhail Gorbachev in *Pravda*, a Soviet daily newspaper, is extensively quoted. Mr. Gorbachev calls for an end to the arms' race and for a major reduction in nuclear weapons. I am confident that Jürgen believed, not necessarily accurately, that we in the USA did not have access to this interview. That is why he sent it to me.

(*Pravda*, by the way, means "truth" in English.)

This exchange of articles continued, and Jürgen expressed some opinions about the German Democratic Republic. In May I sent him some "English homework," as I called it. He wrote, "I really liked 'The Other Germany' because the text gives a different view of the GDR. It's objective – and that surprises me." He agrees with the reasons for the building of the Berlin Wall that are summarized in this article. He called this quote from the article, "very factual and actually free of emotion":

> Three and a half million people crossed from East to West between 1949 and 1961. Many were highly trained scientists, technicians, teachers and skilled workers. No nation – especially a nation trying to recover from near destruction – can tolerate such a hemorrhage of talent.

The article also expressed an opinion that East Germany was a police state, which was a major reason for so many people leaving for West Germany. He asks: "Do you really believe we live here in a police state?"

I did believe that. But I need to add here that while none of us ever experienced "police-state harassment," we were very aware of the state security apparatus – the *Staatssicherheitsdienst* - or *Stasi* – that existed in the GDR and the surveillance role it played in East German society.

However, I had expressed to Jürgen earlier that there was much to be admired in the Democratic Republic: a rich cultural history, a relatively high standard of living for a socialist country, and beautiful cities like Leipzig and Dresden, which we had visited. He seemed to appreciate this was how I felt:

In spite of all this, it would really make me happy if all Americans had such a realistic view of "the other Germany."

Also in this letter Jürgen expresses an opinion about possible unification of the two Germanys: "I don't believe in a 'unification' of 'East and West Germany.' That will not happen in the near future."

He continues, however, writing:

> I'm not of the opinion that the two Germanys coexist as rather reluctant rivals. The most recent Leipzig trade fair showed that the FRG and the GDR are interested in mutual relations, especially in the area of trade.

He is proud of what East Germany had accomplished:

> One thing needs to be said: Our country has existed for only 35 years, it's really something quite new, what we're doing here, and there's no doubt we've made some mistakes. We've accomplished a lot that we are very proud of and there's still a lot to do. In these years we've worked our way up and belong now (you could read it!) to the top ten of all industrialized countries on Earth. And our standard of living is the highest of all socialist countries.

1984 was the year of the Olympic games in Los Angeles, and Jürgen expresses an opinion, which was most likely rather typical in the socialist countries, of the Olympic flame.

> I find it regrettable that the International Olympic Committee

of Greece isn't willing to have the flame lit in Hain of Olympia because the flame is to be used for commercial purposes in the USA. (More and more I feel this way, but I think it makes a lot of sense to be able to exchange my thoughts with you.) As a sportsman, do you think the flame should be sold? What's your opinion?

I actually had no opinion on the topic of the Olympic flame.

Earlier I had offered to continue sending Jürgen articles that would be of interest to him. He responded by saying, "There is no material available about Los Angeles. I would be really interested in information about the city and sport venues. You could really do me a favor!"

It appears to have been very difficult to get information about the USA in East Germany. But when some was available, it was greatly appreciated: "The two texts you sent me I've already loaned to ten students because there's such a demand for them. We don't have here any direct way to learn how the GDR is viewed in the USA."

I had also sent him a text entitled "A Course Description: Politics and the Arts in the GDR." It discussed the East German authors, whose works were available to be read in the USA, at that time. After listing the American authors who were readily available in East Germany - Faulkner, Hemingway, O. Henry, Edgar Allen Poe, Katherine Anne Porter, Philip Roth, who "belong to our literary everyday life here" – Jürgen wrote: "It makes me really happy to hear that there are such courses available over there in which students can read East German authors." He was pleased that American students could read Christa Wolf, Ulrich Plenzdorf, Volker Braun, Heiner Müller, Peter Hacks and Reiner Kunze. However, not with Wolf Biermann, a well-known singer/song-writer:

> Biermann, for example, was hardly known here until he immigrated to the Federal Republic. Since then he merely produces anti-GDR propaganda and has lost his chance to find any recognition here... Otherwise the program is very much like that of educators here and that is very satisfying.

He concludes this letter by writing he was "full of praise and I hope that makes you a little happy, too. So – I think that's enough comment from me of the two texts you sent. The first part (individual propaganda) is not meant to be mean, and I hope you don't read it that way."

I didn't.

Jürgen continues with a description of his academic program at the University of Leipzig:

> The school year is almost over. After June 3 we're going to Weimar for some apprenticeship training. I always discover something new there. But before we go, I still have to pass my examinations. One is on West German literature, the other on literary theory, which gives me some angst. Those two are oral. My written exam is on Marxism/Leninism and their relationship to the scientific theory of communism.

And in conclusion, a very nice statement of his hope for

continued contact:

> So – please excuse all my typos, but if I had written this out longhand you would have hardly been able to read anything. I hope you've understood me and this leads to a nice pen pal relationship.

It did – and that relationship still exists forty years later.

In late September of 1984 Jürgen wrote his first comment to me about wanting to be able to visit California. I had written to him that a fellow Leipzig seminar participant from England had visited us. His reply was, "That David L was with you makes me a little envious – but some day it will happen, that I can also visit you. But even though I couldn't fly to the USA I was still far from home: in Moscow."

(Finally – one of my friends was able to visit the Soviet Union!)

> I'd written to you that I had applied to take a trip to the USSR and on 4 September it finally came to pass. We – student friends and I - were able to visit a great many sites in Moscow: the Kremlin, the "convent of the virgins," churches and chapels, Red Square, the Lenin Mausoleum, St. Basil's cathedral, the cosmonaut memorial, and the exhibition of the "Economic Achievements of the Peoples of the USSR."

> My impressions of the "capital of the world," as Ernest Hemingway once wrote, are the best. I would have liked to have stayed in Moscow longer, I liked it so well. Next year I'd love to go to Leningrad, but it costs quite a bit of money, and as a student I'm not exactly rich.

Jürgen was also in the People's Republic of Poland in 1984 with a seminar group from the University of Leipzig. They conducted a language course for Polish students who were studying German.

> It was very interesting because we otherwise don't have the opportunity to travel to Poland. And the Polish students asked questions, as you do, like almost after every sentence from us: "And that's really your hard and fast opinion?" Or "You really believe that?" They were always so very mistrustful. We were often of different opinions, sometimes discussing until dawn or even longer.

(He does not mention the Solidarity Movement, led by Lech Walesa, which was becoming stronger in the mid-80s.)

His group then visited Krakow where he had more contact with Polish students.

> This was a great experience. By going there we got to know many wonderful people. And that's always most important: meeting other people and exchanging thoughts with them. This made the summer most worthwhile – much like the summer when you guys were here in Leipzig.

Earlier in 1984 I had sent him an article wherein Uwe Gerig, an East German photojournalist who had defected to West Germany in 1983, wrote rather stinging criticism of the GDR. The article was entitled "German-German Hopes." Here are some of Jürgen's comments on what Mr. Gerig had written:

I've hardly read anything worse. I'm against people who leave our country and then cast dirt on the GDR from West Germany – that's the only way I can describe this nonsense. I have no sympathy for these people because all they seem to want to do is emigrate and spit such nonsense at us.

I hope you don't have a bad impression of me or that I'm being impolite – but the text from Gerig really pissed me off. I read it again and still can't change my opinion. There's just so much in there that simply isn't true. "Say nothing, hear nothing, see nothing."– That's not part of what goes on here. I can, for example, express my opinion any time I want. Since I'm a student at the university I can always use and express my opinions.

But if for Gerig free expression means I can stand on any street corner and yell: "Socialism is shit" (Excuse me, please), then he's got the wrong idea of the concept of "freedom" and I must admit that such activity is not permitted here.

Gerig had written that he was "ashamed of his guilt for the conditions of the GDR." Jürgen writes that Gerig doesn't have to be ashamed:

We just renounce him. Either I'm for something or I'm against it. If I'm against it, then I would not pull myself back into the "inner migration," as Gerig does. If I pull myself back into my "private four walls"– seeing nothing, hearing nothing, saying nothing– that is not taking part in any type of social life.

Jürgen's opinion is that Gerig himself was the one who had pulled back into his own "private four walls." It is in this context that he refers to the arms race in Europe:

Gerig doesn't need to concern himself with what's built here or with our future. He should be much more concerned about his own future. He's certainly pulled himself back within his "four walls" as the mid-range rockets are stationed in West Germany and are ready to be used. If the rockets had not been stationed, then the socialist countries would not have been compelled to take such counter measures; if the West hadn't stationed the rockets, the socialist countries wouldn't have had to respond in kind.

Reflecting back and on a personal note, the nuclear arms' race was a major topic of discussions that took place during my weeks in Leipzig in 1983: How did we get into this mess? Several of my journal entries describe interaction with fellow teachers from *both* sides of the Iron Curtain, with students and faculty from the University of Leipzig. They all had a common theme: How did we get into such a dangerous situation, and how do we get out of it? The *people* simply want peace and a future where all countries can co-exist peacefully.

Back to Uwe Gerig. Jürgen writes: "I can only agree with one sentence: 'Our hope lies with the young people… perhaps they have more courage than we do…' "

And where did the peaceful demonstrations begin that led to the fall of the Berlin Wall in November of 1989? In Leipzig. With thousands of young people.

Also in this letter from the summer of 1984 are some interesting comments on the elections in the USA:

We saw here a TV broadcast from West Germany about election campaign events in the USA. And what I saw, dear David, was a fanaticism that cannot be exaggerated. I saw women who broke into tears and screamed when they saw their candidate. One certainly needs to evaluate what one sees, but I'm thinking it's typical of the way things are there. (You certainly don't want to hear that, do you?)

I'm not sure whom the women were crying for: Ronald Reagan or Walter Mondale; but it is worth noting that Jürgen could get Western TV in Leipzig in 1984.

The Olympic Games of 1984 took place in Los Angeles. As one may recall, the USA boycotted the 1980 Moscow games because of the Soviet invasion of Afghanistan. The Soviets, reciprocating, did not take part in the 1984 Games, citing commercialization and lack of security for the athletes. This harks back to Jürgen's comments of the commercialization of the Olympic flame:

Does the Olympic flame have to be sold in order "to bring in donations," as you write? Isn't the government responsible for the institutions of sport as well as for society? Those are certainly points of discussion we could argue about.

Regarding the "Olympic question," which we've already discussed, I can't really add any more that what I said weeks ago. Also, if the USA team had been in Moscow, the Soviets still wouldn't have gone to Los Angeles. That is fact. It wasn't revenge.

I think most Americans called it revenge.

He also writes that the two of us could agree on something:

51

But you're certainly right – it's all very regrettable. And the winning of gold medals is only one aspect, the other certainly being the coming together of athletes and participation in such an event. On this point I agree with you completely. It's just so important.

And definitely it was a great event for the city, as it was for Moscow four years ago.

Jürgen's opinion of Americans' knowledge of the GDR is also worth mentioning here:

And you don't need to contradict me; there are very few people in the States who have a halfway realistic knowledge of the GDR, as you will soon have of the Soviet Union. [I was planning a trip to the Soviet Union in the summer of 1986.] I'm sure you will like it as much as you did here.

It's too bad so few people in the USA don't have a realistic picture of us. Too many just believe blindly what Reagan says. That's what we typically believe here about Americans.

I believe to a certain extent he was right.

Jürgen concludes this letter with a rather long and interesting PS. I had written asking for his opinion of Erich Honecker (communist party chief of the GDR) turning down an invitation to visit West Germany. His explanation:

I don't think this decision was directly influenced by the Soviets, but much more that the decision was Honecker's alone. Naturally we don't want to have any illusions – our politics are closely related to those of the Warsaw Pact countries.

West German politicians are really lacking when it comes to diplomatic sensitivities. It just can't be that a politician such as Federal Chancellor Kohl says on West German TV that he won't listen to topics that simply don't interest him. And one doesn't have to think very long as to what those topics are!

So – what is Honecker supposed to do when Kohl says he doesn't want to listen to him?

And certainly many remarks made in the West German Parliament, which were directed against Honecker, play a role here. I think the whole thing is not accidental, but much more as planned attacks by the opposition to hinder real negotiations and dialog. And most of all, Alfred Dregger must be mentioned, exactly as in the text you sent. [Dregger was a very conservative West German Politician who proposed outlawing the Communist Party in West Germany.]

For the first time in his letters there is something one might call criticism, albeit very small, of the Soviet Union:

On the other hand, I'm disappointed that such decisions give the Soviets more credit. Honecker, in my opinion, is sovereign enough to make such decisions.

* * *

Other than personal topics such as education, jobs, family life, and travel, there was one topic seemed to dominate our correspondence: Peace. The decade of the 80s was, one might say, the "high point" of the Cold War. The West, was led by the United States and joined together through the North Atlantic Treaty Organization; the East, was dominated by the Soviet

Union and tied together through the Warsaw Pact. These two alliances faced off against each other with thousands of nuclear weapons. Both sides basically had the same motto: "An attack on one is an attack on all." If that nuclear exchange had ever occurred, civilization as we knew it would likely have ended.

East Germans, living in a small country right between these two power blocks, were naturally very worried about what could happen. They would have never started the war. But if it ever did start, they knew they had no chance of survival. Many times my friends in the German Democratic Republic all expressed their concern about this precarious situation.

Jürgen writes in December, 1984: "I got your, as you say, 'peace items.' Thank you very much for them – I can make good use of them in my preparations for English class."

I was active during these years in an organization called Beyond War. Our purpose was to educate fellow Americans about the true dangers of nuclear war. This sentence sums up the purpose of Beyond War: "If we work together, we can realize a world without war."

I had sent Jürgen some Beyond War materials. In December he writes:

> It was again very interesting to read "something American" dealing with the most serious topic we face on the entire planet today – that of peace. And I wish that the Beyond War movement will have many members, that is, enough members,

so that in the 85th year of this century peace will be maintained and that a nuclear inferno will be avoided. It's good that so many people are supposed to be reached – 7.5 million. That's a lot, especially when you consider the population of the GDR. [Sixteen million in 1990.]

Another issue I brought up in my "Beyond War letter" was the restrictions on East Germans who wanted to travel to the Soviet Union. I asked him his opinion on why this was so. His reply:

Naturally I can't give you a good answer as to why the Soviets maintain such a policy and no other. I mean their policy regarding contact with foreigners. I've also wondered about that. When I was in Moscow last summer I met nothing but open, loving, peace-loving and good-of-heart people. They were all so happy to have contact with me.

It seemed, however, that personal contact was not approved. While in Moscow, Jürgen wanted to visit a Russian woman from the Leipzig seminar whom we both knew.

I was not able to make any contact with Emilya. I never got a reply from her. Perhaps the letter was lost in the mail. A similar thing happened to a friend who wanted to visit an acquaintance in Moscow – always no response. We think such contacts are just not allowed – don't ask me why, though. But unfortunately, that's the way it is.

I also traveled to the Soviet Union with my son Tim, but not until the summer of 1986: A train journey from Moscow to

Irkusk in Siberia, flying back to Uzbekistan and then on to Leningrad. I had mentioned to Jürgen about the possibility of seeing Emilya, who lived in Novosibirsk. He continues:

> And this lets me answer your question about your going to Novosirbirsk. You won't have any problem, in so far that you have the opportunity of going there. But no way should you go there without informing Emiliya first. You most certainly have to do that. Otherwise, she could get into real trouble. So just wait and see what she says.
>
> It would be best if you sent her a registered letter; they get to their destination quicker. And send two letters, just in case one of them gets lost. Yeah – that's about all the advice I'd have. But try it, it's not easy.

I didn't write her, and I did not try to visit her. But Tim and I had a fascinating trip.

CHAPTER SIX

1985

I had mentioned earlier to Gerhard about the trip to Siberia and that maybe he could join us. In April 1985, he wrote such a trip would not be for him:

> I was at the Soviet and German travel bureaus and only got stupid answers. The brochures only deal with Siberia in general and not with any specific trips. I'd really like to go along, but I don't want to spend so much money traveling to a country that doesn't seem to like me at all. There are so many regulations and restrictions there that one can't move about freely, and can't get to know people because they are so afraid to reach out and make any contact.

He also writes about the difficulty he was having in obtaining electronic goods. "Think ahead of time," he wrote, "of what you could bring me."

Our mutual friend Linda had brought him a Walkman:

> I really wanted a small radio. I would have never guessed it was so expensive for her.

> I'm very interested in electronic technology. I've bought two headsets for my big system here – but they just don't live up to my expectations as to what a true stereo experience should be.

I'm happy with the speakers, but my neighbors just don't like to hear my music through the walls. The headset would have to have an impedance of 300 ohm and if possible a European plug with five outlets. Don't worry if you can't find the right adaptor: Perhaps I could make myself one ahead of time – I've got kind of a hobby tinkering with electronic stuff.

(This turned out to be very true, as we shall see when we learn how he was making some money in 2011.)

Gerhard became a regular listener to AFN, the American Forces' Network.

My favorite radio station is AFN because they play music all day long that I really like. And political shows on West German TV interest me the most because our country is so small that one is just compelled to find out what is going on in other countries.

Gerhard concludes this letter by writing about how difficult it was in the GDR to "deal with anything foreign." For example, cashing a check: Linda had sent him a check for $35 so he could buy her a Christmas nutcracker, which were hand-made in East Germany. Not so easy to do:

I went with this check from bank to bank, but nobody knew how to begin to cash it. Finally I found a bank that could do something with it – but they gave me no cash just some checks that I would have to use in an Intershop. [Intershops were stores where only foreign currency could be used to buy goods that were not available in "normal" East German shops. And the Christmas nutcrackers would not be available until the Christmas season.] She'll just have to wait a little.

He concluded with more information about "things foreign." And that included us, his American friends:

> It really surprises me that you guys can visit me without problems, and that normally the mail takes 20 days – but we've just got to live with that. To my surprise I've never noticed that any of the mail from the USA has been opened. Only the letter with Linda's $20 cash never got here. I guess that's just the way things are, and we've got to live with it.

Or maybe we just should not send cash.

Included with this letter were more newspaper clippings, which gave an indication of how the state-run newspapers wanted the West to be viewed. The articles dealt with: Crime in New York; a dog getting elected honorary mayor Sunol, California; a TASS [the Soviet news agency] article on a suspected US Army- sponsored break-in at a Soviet military outpost in East Germany; the US increasing pressure on New Zealand to allow nuclear powered ships to dock; the US military threatens Nicaragua with military intervention.

I'm not saying these events did not happen, only that the East German press often focused its reporting on such events during the 1980s.

* * *

On July 1, 1985 Jutta's son was born! Her letter of July 4th reveals how proud she was: "I'm happy to tell you the good news: at about 9 pm our son DAVID [happy face] was born!" I was about to burst with pride that the baby was named after me. But: "Nevertheless, I have to calm down your pride – it isn't <u>you</u> personally who influenced the choice of the name."

Darn!

She continues with a very interesting and sensitive comment, when put into an historical context:

> I have a special inclination to Hebrew names, and maybe it's more over a confession to Jews as the German "Schwarzen Schafe" [black sheep, in English] of history. Besides, I really love the sound of Jewish names.

In this same letter she mentions Beyond War, the peace organization in which I was active. "Write me more about 'Beyond War' and send me some information! I'm always interested in such things."

Jutta continued with these references to current events of the mid-80s:

> An American girlfriend of mine writes me about American policy, too. She's very much engaged in contacts in Nicaragua, and moreover she works in a sanctuary for Guatemalan refugees who are on the run throughout their lives. There's much stupidity and cruelty in the world – and the most dangerous thing is the connection of both of them. Look at the Nazis and you know what I mean. Almost whole Latin America supports people like the concentration camp doctor Josef Mengele. [Mengele was able to live in South America (Argentina, Paraguay, and Brazil) until his death in 1979].

These countries gave him a chance to survive, though he was one of the most sadistic murderers Hitler ever had.

Jutta's concluding sentence in this letter is: "Let's survive; let humanity survive!"

Need she say more?

* * *

Barbara, the university student and close friend of Jürgen, met Ivan and me at the Leipzig train station on July 5, 1983, the day before our institute began. I never really got to know her well during my weeks at the language institute, but because of her connection with Jürgen we became somewhat acquainted and eventually began to write to each other. It actually took a couple of years before we corresponded on a regular basis. The facilitator for this exchange of letters was Jürgen.

Two of their letters written on the same day, October 9, 1985, address the same topic: Jürgen writes, "I'll have to reprimand Barbara because she hasn't written to you yet." He had been communicating with her, verified by what she also wrote:

Jürgen told me today that my letter to you from June or July apparently didn't arrive. I'm sorry, because I happily sat one evening for a really long time late into the night writing by candlelight at my desk.

And write she did.

We corresponded quite regularly over the next three years. I hope my English translations of her letters do justice to her German.

> Your card with the crystal blue skies from Ivan's hometown [La Jolla, California] stood for a long time on my desk. Your letter really made me happy because such a long time has passed since the summer institute. I actually think of it quite often still because the pleasant give-and-take between nations and cultures was such a nice thing — so uncomplicated and covering so many topics.

She was still a full-time student at the University of Leipzig in the fall of 1985, and this letter gives us some good information on university student life in East Germany.

But, almost as an aside, she writes she had met "THE man", a merchant seaman about to go to sea to India. This was not going to get in the way of her studies: "And while he's on his journey I'm working on my thesis. My tenth and last semester I'll be at Humboldt University in Berlin."

Humboldt was the major university in East Berlin during the years of the German Democratic Republic. Today it is still one of the finest universities in Europe.

By studying in Berlin, Barbara could finish her studies sooner:

> I'm trying to do that because in Berlin there are many famous people from the German Academy of Sciences teaching there – and that opens many opportunities before the door closes.

Once finished with her undergraduate work, she planned to continue her studies in Leipzig in the field of German literature of the Federal Republic, Switzerland and Austria.

> In three years I'll write my dissertation on post-1945 Swiss poetry; that is the next station to which I'm striving. Where that will lead me professionally I don't know – but I don't want to remain in Leipzig. Eight years are enough, I think.

Barbara preferred studying in East Berlin much more than in Leipzig: "Student life in Berlin just appeals to me a lot more than in provincial Leipzig." She favored the life-style she found in Prenzlauerberg, an East Berlin suburb:

> It's a part of Berlin where the old fluidity of Berlin just continues. With some tricks some old friends of mine and I were able to get an apartment. Every evening we really got it going.

Berlin did "flow," even in the East, during the 1980s: restaurants, street cafes, bars, nightclubs, discos, parks, theater, and music. Not as "lively" as West Berlin, of course, but still preferable to Leipzig for Barbara.

Her admiration for Berlin is illustrated by what she wrote about the city itself.

But first, allow me a short German lesson: The German word for "capital city" is *Hauptstadt*, with *Haupt* meaning "head" or "chief" and *Stadt* meaning "city." Therefore, Berlin is the *Hauptstadt* of Germany.

Barbara is referring, of course, to East Berlin, the capital of the Democratic Republic: "Berlin is truly 'Haupt-stadt' and center. We've got many beautiful corners in our country, but when one experiences the 'certain something' of Berlin, it's just incomparable."

I agree with her – Berlin *is* a special place.

Barbara asks in this letter for information and some personal feelings from me.

> What were your impressions of Berlin and overall of the young people in the GDR? And don't try to flatter me! I'm not narrow-minded. I'm really interested in a purely factual way what is said about us in the "land of infinite possibilities" [the USA], as it's always called, a land that is always interested primarily in itself.

That was a very interesting comment, I thought. How could one *ever* accuse the USA of "self-interest?"

> And has your country recovered from Boris Becker [tennis star from West Germany] fever yet? Right now all of Europe is holding its breath over the qualification for the Davis Cup final. It's funny how such things can make borders disappear.

I honestly do not remember what I wrote back to her regarding her question about my overall impressions of the GDR. But, now looking back on forty years of contact with these individuals, my time in East Germany led me to a genuine appreciation for the lives of people who were doing their best to get educated, make the most of their situations, travel – albeit with major restrictions – and eventually, as the 1980s drew to a close, become involved in a peaceful revolution; only four years later the Wall would fall, and the Cold War would soon end.

Barbara concludes her letter with a compliment and a greeting from Germany in the fall:

> I've got a lot of confidence in your knowledge of German – therefore I've written things just as they came to mind, not worrying about complicated expressions – please forgive me, if I've come across a little crass. I'd really like to hear from you again. Here is a greeting from the wonderfully beautiful and warm fall we're having this year.

Attached to her letter was a small yellow and brown leaf from the fall of 1985 in East Germany.

Very nice and very much appreciated.

* * *

Now back to Jürgen's letter of the same day as Barbara's, October 9, 1985: He reflects back on our getting together earlier that year in Berlin:

> It's been exactly eleven weeks since we met in Berlin. Walter [a close friend of his] and I think very often of this time together. It was simply wonderful.

I so much want to meet again, but I doubt it can happen. It's really too bad that you live so far from Europe – one never knows if we'll ever get together again. And it makes me a little sad when you write that you'll be doing another tour to Europe, but won't be coming to the GDR. I can't come to London or Paris. So a future meeting is uncertain. Too bad!

But Jürgen also wrote that life in the GDR was not horrible, even with the restrictions on travel freedoms. After our meeting in East Berlin, he then spent some time in Mecklenburg, a pleasant rural area in the northern part of East Germany.

We visited my parents there in their cabin. It was just fantastic. We went for long rides in the paddleboat, took a ten hour trip in the motorboat, collected mushrooms we could eat and did a lot of hiking.

Unfortunately this vacation was much too short. We had to return to Leipzig because the semester began again.

My studies are coming to an end. Each week we have only four classes – that's really not much. The rest of the time we spend writing our papers as well as preparing for the examination in literary history. That will be a very difficult exam, but it's the last one.

Earlier I had sent Jürgen an article dealing with East-West relations and the prospects for peace. I'm happy he found it informative and useful, for he spends the rest of this letter telling me about how he was able to use this article in a class:

I wanted to write more about my studies, because the article you sent me relates to what we're studying: At the beginning of each year we have an introductory week in which our seminar groups meet; we talk about politics, world peace and our hopes. And you can certainly imagine that Walter and I had so much to talk about, because we were the only ones in our group who've had the opportunity to talk with "real" Americans, that is, to come into "skin-close" contact with another ideology.

The class had a very interesting title: *Yalta-Potsdam-Helsinki. Actual lessons of the struggle for disarmament and peace.* This is another example of how great a concern there was in East Germany about the dangers of the arms' race. Jürgen writes in more detail about what the students in this class discussed and analyzed: "Naturally we came again and again to the preference of the USA to station weapons in space."

The "weapons in space" were President Reagan's Strategic Defense Initiative, commonly known as SDI. It caused great concern, not only in Europe, but also to a certain extent in the USA. It was a weapons' system that would intercept Soviet intercontinental ballistic missile warheads before they could re-enter the atmosphere. How expensive would it be? Could it ever really work? Those were the two main questions also being asked in the USA.

And I don't know if you remember that when we were in Berlin, we briefly spoke about the Strategic Defense Initiative, and you said you were convinced that there would be no weapons in space. And I say to you today that SDI will exist.

In our seminar, we listed the weapons' systems that have been

67

developed since the construction of the atomic bomb. And today one has to conclude that since then there has been a continuity of the development of always more dangerous weapons' systems; the self-perpetuation of weapons naturally leads to the necessity of even newer weapons. And therefore SDI will certainly be the beginning of all this, and we see its purpose as keeping the battlefield as far away as possible from the USA.

And why won't this work, and why won't it be safe? Computers, according to Jürgen:

Computer games might be a lot of fun and have a certain charm, but when computers control these weapons, and they have a tendency to make mistakes. Then the apocalypse isn't far off. Right?

Jürgen continues with his opinion as to where hope lies: Western Europe.

But pessimism doesn't help us to move on. Our hope lies not lastly with the powers in Western Europe. Many Western European nations are against SDI, against the most powerful of NATO and against the interests of the USA. It can be determined that these nations are making great efforts to become more strongly integrated through the European Union. And this is because they want to create a different relationship to the USA. (They want to become more united, not vassals!)

A common criticism from the East Bloc of the USA during the Cold War was that the weapons' program was simply being pushed to promote economic progress. Jürgen explained it this way:

> What I actually think is that what Reagan's trying to do, is that with such expenditures for armaments a certain standard of living in the USA can be maintained. Things are going pretty well for the average American, aren't they? But what disturbs me, to a certain extent, what makes me sad, and makes me a little pessimistic, is the fact that the average American doesn't care what the costs are to maintain his standard of living. Do you understand what I mean?

I did – but I also think that at that time Jürgen really didn't know how many Americans were actually against SDI and the constant development of weapons.

However, maybe some good did come out of the USA's pushing the arms race. To be completely honest in an historical perspective, one must admit that President Reagan's weapons' program played a major role in the fall of the Soviet Union. They just could not afford to keep up, Gorbachev knew that, changes were made, and by 1992 the Soviet Empire had fallen.

And this scenario is almost predicted by Jürgen in this letter. I had sent him an article with a summary of a press conference President Reagan held, wherein he stated that he was optimistic about the prospects for an end to the arms' race. Jürgen's comment:

> Perhaps there is hope. I just ask myself, where is it supposed to come from? From Washington? From Moscow? Have you seen Gorbachev's new disarmament suggestions? That's one

thing that makes me optimistic. It remains to be seen, though, how Reagan will react. Will he just call it a propaganda stunt?

Jürgen includes a cartoon from an East German newspaper. It shows an American politician saying: "We'll test the latest disarmament suggestions of the Soviets – and we'll immediately know they will be against them." The criticism being that in the USA the disarmament suggestions of the Soviets are never being taken seriously.

Jürgen's comment: "I think this hits the nail on the head. . . . Enough of politics. Otherwise this letter will never end."

This rather long letter concludes with a couple of personal comments that I thought were quite nice and, shall we say, honest:

> I'm also sending you the pictures of our get-together in Berlin. I've made some duplicates – you can give them to your students who were there. I really like those kids. The best of greetings to all! And I'm expecting a long letter from you. Don't let me wait too long – earlier you were writing almost every week.

I can't remember how long I made him wait until my next letter – but our correspondence still continues; as I write this it's July of 2014.

* * *

Christmas, 1985. Jutta wishes my family and me a "healthy

and fulfilled New Year;" our exchange of *Frohe Weihnachten* continues to this day. Her 1985 Christmas card continues with the following quote from East German author Christa Wolf, which, to me, encapsulates how Jutta views the future:

"When we stop hoping, what we fear will certainly come."

Jutta never gave up hope that there would be changes in the German Democratic Republic. And, as we know, things really did begin to change three years later, in the fall of 1989.

David F. Strack

The Wall in Later Years

Checkpoint Charlie crossing, looking toward East Berlin.

No-man's-land between East Berlin apartments and the Wall

Another view of no-man's-land behind the Wall.

Brandenburg Gate viewed from the West.

Newer Wall had rounded top to prevent grappling.

A memorial to some of those who died trying to escape over the Wall.

Wall graffiti mocking 35 year anniversary of East Germany.

Palace of Tears, where the author often said goodbye to his East German friends.

Sculpture representing the division of Berlin into four sections after WWII.

The GDR border station at Checkpoint Charlie in the 1980s.

CHAPTER SEVEN

1986

The first letter I received in 1986 is dated January 22nd. It's from Jürgen, in Leipzig. He writes about his studies and having just finished the semester's study: "Finally everything is over; I had my last test yesterday – the state exam in literary science." It was difficult and he got a grade of 3, which would equate to a C+/B- or so, in the American system. He "hadn't even dreamed of that grade. We've been celebrating since yesterday – and we have reason to. My good friend Walter got a *One!*" (That's an A+.) Jürgen would then have no academic work until April, when a major paper was due.

And speaking of studying and school, I had, for some reason, also sent him pictures of my German classroom at Yucaipa High School; they were just photos of the room itself and the bulletin boards. His reaction to seeing these made my day, so to speak:

> I got your letter with the photos. They are just wonderful! Walter and I got such a kick out of them. We loved the photos of your classroom. It would be simply unimaginable to have such a colorful classroom here! Your bulletin board with "YHS ACTIVITIES" is just incredible. We discovered our picture

there. What a feeling! We are hanging on your bulletin board.

I was proud to have a picture of my East German friends in my classroom. I hope it was a small part in showing my students that there were "real" people in communist East Germany.

Jürgen and Walter also saw a printed sign that was posted: "But the best was *Hose zu?* Do you know what that means?"

Of course I did. It means in English: "Is your fly zipped?"

"One could never hang that on a wall here," was Jürgen's comment about one little vocabulary lesson my students were "exposed" to.

They also noticed something else:

Impressive was your beer coaster collection that we could see on the top of the chalkboard. Does such a thing always belong to classroom equipment in the USA? I always thought you guys just learned there. I can just imagine that it must be fun to learn in this classroom.

Of course we didn't drink any beer, but I do hope it was fun to learn in my classroom.

Earlier I had sent Jürgen a backpack, and in this letter he thanked me most sincerely. I really didn't know how much this "gift" was appreciated until I read this:

I've got to thank you a thousand times over – the backpack arrived. Do you know what I did? A long time ago you sent me a small flag of the California Republic. I've sewed this right in the middle and it looks wonderful. Since then it's the only bag

I carry – it's always with me. So – many thanks, it got here safe and sound.

Before concluding this letter, he writes his New Year's greeting:

> It's just occurred to me that I haven't extended the best of New Year's wishes to the USA. Herewith they are extended. I wish all of you – you and your family – all the best for 1986. Stay healthy and happy.

He apologizes for our not being able to meet in Berlin that coming summer: "But I've got some not so good news. You write about your possible stop in Berlin."

I had written to him indicating that I was planning a trip with my older son, Tim, to the Soviet Union in August, with a possible stop in Berlin. We made the trip, but did not stop in Berlin.

The reason for Jürgen's not being able to be in Berlin was that he had received permission, finally, to go to the Soviet Union:

> In February I'll probably learn for sure that Walter and I will be in the Soviet Union for five weeks, in Tashkent, in the Uzbek SSR [Soviet Socialist Republic]. We'll work there and then make a trip through the Soviet Union. I've been looking forward to this for such a long time and finally got permission.

As it turned out, we just missed each other in Tashkent. Our trip took my son and me eventually to Tashkent, after traveling from Moscow to Irkutsk in Siberia by train, and then flying to Uzbekistan, before moving on to Leningrad.

I really appreciated how Jürgen finished this letter:

> So, David, it's already very late and we want to celebrate a little. I've written such bad German today with much *ja, je, nun, also, so,* and *na.*

These words are called "flavoring particles" in German, and have most often no direct meaning in English. It was not bad German at all – it was another very nice letter from a friend in the German Democratic Republic.

* * *

Let's continue with correspondence from Barbara.

In February of 1986, she writes about restrictions on travel that she was still experiencing:

> That we don't have complete freedom to travel is something I don't like – like most people here. Political reasons from the sixties are the reason for the closing of the borders.

History tells us the reason for this – the construction of the Berlin Wall and the closed border with West Germany - was the East German government's fear that so many important and educated people such as doctors, professors, teachers, engineers, scientists, and normal working citizens would eventually leave East Germany for the West. As we read earlier in one of Gerhard's letters, such a situation could not be tolerated if the Democratic Republic were to survive as a socialist state and Soviet satellite country.

By 1960 this exodus to the West had become a major problem for the Democratic Republic.

Berlin was from where people could "easily" flee. One could walk, drive, take a tram or the subway into West Berlin and then travel by train or plane, possibly even by car, to West Germany. It was also very dangerous to attempt to leave over the border between the two countries because it was a barbed-wire fortification heavily patrolled and guarded by watch towers, each within the sight of another. But it could be done from East Berlin to West Berlin. To stop the flow, the building of the Wall began on August 13, 1961.

Barbara described how travel restrictions were loosening a bit in 1986:

But today… We have become so big that for us nothing seems unnatural, but eventually the desire to see more, which is something completely natural, comes. Some possibilities – very few with tourism, but, for example, we already have youth exchanges and youth tour groups to Scandinavia, West Germany, France and other European countries.

And then travels with special permission for family members are also possible – my father spent four days in West Berlin for his mother's birthday.

She continues by describing in more detail who was being allowed to travel to the West:

> Travel mostly has to do with work: transit, sea travel, scientific exchanges, educational support in Africa, Vietnam, construction, repairs. We've had all that for a while. It's really not too much. But in contrast to ten years ago it's progress.

In her next sentence – remember, this letter was written in 1986 – Barbara uses a word that became one of the most important words in the German language in the late 1980s: *Wende*.

Here's the sentence where she used that word for the first time. I had never seen it used in that context: "There are further negotiations with some countries, and I hope that a *Wende* for better times will take place."

This word in English can mean "reversal" or "turning point." A *Wende* can also be a change in direction. *Wende* became the word used in German for the "revolution" of 1989 – and Barbara is using it in 1986, not in any great context of a revolution, but in an expression of hope for better times to come.

Little did she know how important that word would become for all of Germany just three years later!

The following clearly sums up Barbara's feelings of what was happening in East Germany in 1986:

For many it's not the concept of the "Golden West" – but people let themselves be spoiled. There's nowhere on Earth where everything is perfect. Everything has advantages and disadvantages; each system produces positive things and bad – sometimes more, sometimes less.

I grew up here and am rooted here – couldn't live anywhere else because I know I'd get homesick. But I still want to TRAVEL and SEE. Others have no understanding of the restrictions we are under. That's a basic disadvantage that I have while living here. I'll never give up the hope that the borders will someday be open – Jürgen and Walter certainly also.

They had to wait nearly four more years: On November 9, 1989, the borders opened and her wish came true.

East Germany, throughout the 1970s and 1980s, was known as a small nation that produced very fine athletes, particularly at the Olympic level. One need only mention Katarina Witt, the world-renowned figure skater.

Barbara, while never participating at the national level, was quite an active athlete during her pre-college years. In her letter of February, 1986, she writes about how important athletics were in her life and in the lives of other young people. It seems that the "gifted" athletes were chosen by school or state authorities, not like in the USA where parental pressure might play a much larger role.

Here is what Barbara wrote about athletics in the GDR:

Gifted children are chosen very early in their school years. Size, results on specialized tests, and performance are all important. Then they're trained with specific goals. For young people we have many sport clubs and institutions available: soccer, volleyball, swimming, team handball, gymnastics; track and field are the most popular.

One might ask, "Which system is better?" An advantage I see of the socialist system is that the truly gifted athletes, while pushed and forced to work very hard, get to travel and have experiences that the "non-athlete" will not. But having coached several sports – tennis, basketball, football, and soccer – at the high school level, I believe the "parental pressure" issue is not that great of a problem in our youth sport programs. Being an athlete at the youth and high school level in the USA, in my opinion, helps develop very well-rounded young people, physically and academically. I'm not sure that was the case in East Germany.

Barbara's top priority was always her academic studies, but being an athlete was still important to her:

When I was 14 or 15 I went four or five times a week to team handball practice, and my friends thought I was crazy. It was fun, though, but it made me a little angry because of all the other stuff I had to give up. Especially on Saturdays when the others were going to a village dance, and I was on the train going to a game – oh, the wasted time on the trains! Or in May during spring break they all got to go camping and hiking, and I had handball camp.

Her handball commitment continued into her college years: "While in college I wasn't able to train at home – I was on the second team and then got to the substitute bench on the first team."

In February after finishing her semester examinations and writing a major term paper, she was able to start training again:

> I'm involved with a team in a county league – that's a middle level of competition. It's for athletes who aren't members of sport clubs. And we're not bad. Because of our studies we're scattered throughout the GDR, but we all work together.
>
> It's not easy though. Travel is done by train because we have no bus. We are usually underway the whole day, what with the transfers. That gets on my nerves. I get very excited for the games, though.

It became obvious that she lived a very active life as a young girl and then as a college student.

Barbara also writes in this letter about her living conditions, which actually seemed quite nice during these years of her life. Her hometown is Luckenwalde, a suburb south of Berlin, and was at that time about 550 years old.

> Some industry, some agriculture, many old apartment blocks, but all-in-all pretty comfortable and pleasant. I like it here very much and don't want to leave.

She and Andreas were planning to build a house in the next couple of years in Löwendorf, a nearby village. She describes the process:

> If one hangs in there long enough to get the proper authorization, then the finances from the state are very possible – even for young people. Only getting the materials can be problematic – one has to actually be kind of lucky. We're going to build our "basic place" in Löwendorf, and then we'll continue with the project.

(In a subsequent letter we'll learn how this project went.)

Fasching– or Carnival– is the German equivalent of Mardi Gras, a time of partying and celebration before Lent begins on Ash Wednesday. Some in the West might have been surprised that such a Christian tradition was "alive and well" in socialist East Germany. Barbara gives us a rather nice description of these traditions in her East German village:

> Right now it's *Fasching* or Carnival here. Do you guys know such a thing? It's originally from an old custom here that was supposed to drive winter away. People got dressed up in order to scare winter away, made music and go really rowdy. In the south and in the countryside much of this still goes on. It's mostly just "crazy days," with crazy stuff going on, people dressing up, celebrating, and, and, and… On November 11 at 11:00 am [11.11.11.00 AM] every year this all starts.

Then a period of normality continues until just before Ash Wednesday, with what the Germans call "Rose Monday" and "Fasting Night."

Barbara gives us a general description: Rose Monday is fun with "its gigantic parades through the streets in Cologne and

Mainz in West Germany and here in Wasungen." Wasungen is still known today as "The Carnival City" and lies west of Leipzig. "Lots of partying goes on in the discos and restaurants until Ash Wednesday when all is passed."

Her description of the activities in a secondary school in the seaside town of Rostock, where Andreas was, gives us more insight into how Carnival is celebrated, even in communist East Germany.

> The school is celebrating its tenth Fasching in a huge way in many rooms for three days. I've made myself a costume bedecked with spiders and spider webs. The theme is "Rumpelkammer," which is a small room where one keeps old stuff that just gets dusty. All has been prepared: a program with the funniest ideas as its theme, the marriage office where one can "marry" for one night... *Fasching* is basically a lot of fun for me, although to a certain extent it's degenerating or boring...

In May I received three letters from East Germany, one each from Jürgen, Barbara and Gerhard.

* * *

Barbara wrote the first on May 11. She was "trying once again" with her typewriter and thanked me for my "beautiful card from Yosemite - many thanks! As always it will hang for some time above my desk and let me dream of such faraway places of this world."

She also hoped we could meet in Berlin before my trip with my son to the Soviet Union that coming July:

> Meeting again this summer in Berlin would make me so very happy. I've got nothing going at the time you mention so it really should work. Let me know the particulars and I'll come for sure.

As I wrote earlier, our itinerary wound up not including Berlin. Too bad.

A huge environmental disaster dominated the news in April of 1986: the meltdown of the nuclear power plant in Tschernobyl, not far from Kiev, capital of the Ukranian Soviet Republic.

Here is what Barbara wrote about the Tschernobyl disaster:

> I hope the panicky reports from Tschernobyl won't scare you away! I've seen in the news that tourism from the USA to Europe has really fallen off because of fear of radiation, terror and war.
>
> I don't want to down play it, but the danger from the burning of the reactor doesn't really exist as it's being portrayed. In the Federal Republic they've closed kindergartens, playgrounds and outdoor swimming pools out of ignorance of what the actual facts are. The informational politics of the Soviet Union are going along with this and are guilty and irresponsible.
>
> But the media and politics of the West are running wild with their speculative comments about the ecological disaster. I just couldn't listen any more – just a bunch of noise. On the radio in the kitchen while doing dishes I heard one thing, on the TV in the living room the opposite.

I then concentrated on what the real experts were saying, which was this: The chief of the West German radiation protection commission said that the checks in all areas (tests at the borders, on food stuffs, water, air and soil) show that the situation in Tschernobyl really is dangerous, but the rest of Europe really isn't seriously affected. Naturally, the readings are above normal, but well under the danger level. International experts at a meeting in Scandinavia said exactly the same thing, and that the radiation levels in the 1960s, during the many above ground nuclear tests, were more dangerous all over the planet – and nobody raised such a stink then.

In my opinion, public pressure, attention, and interest should be much more directed at safety measures in the current nuclear power plants.

She concludes her comments on the disaster with these very pointed sentences:

Care should be directed to those in the Soviet Union who have been directly affected by this – because that's where it's really bad. Instead, dog owners are being asked if they think it's safe on the streets for their little four-legged pets. All of a sudden people are only thinking of their own skin and their spoiled vegetables.

* * *

I'd like to add to Barbara's comments on Tschernobyl by quoting an entry from my journal written on July 31, 1986, while in Moscow. We were staying at the Hotel Cosmos, and had taken a walk outside after dinner, and I met a Russian gentleman. Later that evening, I wrote the following:

I walked outside to get some air and a Russian asked me if the main entrance was the only entrance to the hotel. We then talked for two hours.

He's from Kiev and is in Moscow because of the nuclear accident. Claims it was because of military experiments going on. All in Kiev are very upset about it. "Country of lies." His children, two and five years of age, have been affected. 2,000 people died/will die. He's in Moscow at his mother's – wife and kids are here, too.

Teaches violin – 150 rubles per month. Pays 30 rubles per month rent. Says military expansion down now only because of lousy economy. Whole country lives a lie. "Things are OK, but really aren't."

Gorbachev gave some hope, but Tschernobyl destroyed that. Totalitarian state keeps people down – but most don't resist anyway. Too afraid or too apathetic.

Tschernobyl wasn't the only event of 1986 that Barbara writes about in this letter: The U.S. bombing of Libya on April 15 also caused her great concern. She'd seen the reports on this from West German TV:

And then there's the story of Libya, which in no way has led to an improvement in the situation. It just makes everything worse!

I must say that it really scared me when I saw on TV how many Americans, when surveyed, approved of the strike. Should such shortsightedness really rule people? In the rest of the world – thank God – people think quite differently.

Barbara, like many East Germans – as well as many West

Germans and Americans – was quite vocal in her opposition to the use of weapons and the nuclear arms' race: "I basically cannot condone the use of weapons to solve conflict. And not being a pacifist, it's just not very easy." As others from the GDR did, she had severe criticism of President Reagan:

> Reagan's policies in this regard are dangerous and built on deception. That scares me. I see him as bearing the chief responsibility for the whole situation.

She did, however, believe things might be changing for the better, particularly with the leadership of Mikhail Gorbachev in the Soviet Union.

In Barbara's opinion, the British were an exception to this. They "suffered delusions of grandeur" since their victory in the Falkland Islands and were still saying "yes and amen" to more armaments.

Gorbachev's reforms in the Soviet Union – which were having a positive effect for more freedoms in East Germany – led Barbara to speak quite highly of him:

> I've also got to say that I believe that with Gorbachev there's someone in the government who subjectively and honestly means that he's not pursuing power and the desire for world power and also abstains from this aggressive foreign policy. He rejects the cult of personality, is very realistic, eloquent, and above all, observant and educated. I'm not worried that he will take any non-thought-out and hurried steps (i.e. jumping into Libya, as the fanatical Gadhafi would have liked).

She also expressed her opinion on terrorism. It wasn't "such a big deal here in the East" because "ecological and disarmament questions" were much more important. "We then need to become masters of these through politics and controls."

She concludes this letter as follows:

> Oh, David, what a strenuous and difficult letter this has become! But what is one to do? The world is completely wrapped up in such discussions, almost every conversation, every get-together, is driven by these topics. I'm just so tired of it all – when one is just "a little light," one has no possibilities or chances. But unfortunately, one just can't withdraw oneself.

In 1989 East Germans like Barbara took to the streets with candles to express their goal of *die Wende*, the "change of direction" for East Germany, which actually led to the opening of the Berlin Wall. Yes, she was just "one little light" – one of what would become a river of lights, made up of hundreds of thousands of candles that led the way to a free and democratic East Germany and eventually to a re-united country.

> I would really be interested in what people in your world, on your continent over there, think, and how they deal with all of this. Perhaps a little certainty can come out knowing that. As long as Andreas is underway somewhere in the world where he could be in danger, it just intensifies the whole thing for me.

I regret I have no recollection of what I wrote back in

response to her wanting to know how people in "my world" felt about all of this. I do remember, however, that many of my friends and acquaintances began to be hopeful that the Cold War would soon end. But, in all honesty, we had no idea that the Berlin Wall would fall as soon as it did, in just three years.

* * *

Mid-May, 1986, and Jürgen completes his studies. The concluding academic project for students at the University of Leipzig, as in many German universities, is the "thesis paper." Jürgen submitted his about two weeks before writing:

> It was really quite a bit of work. Mine was 140 pages with index and literary notes. Walter also wrote so much. We are proud of our work – hopefully it all pays off.

> We then had reason to celebrate, as students do. It's the absolute highpoint of one's studies – the thesis. It was quite a week: we celebrated for the entire week, each day in another place with much beer and wine.

> The last thing we have to do is defend our papers. But we know what we've written and are therefore not afraid of this "test." So now we've got some time until September to recover and take some time off for vacation.

Jürgen's studies in German and German literature led to his becoming employed by a publishing company in Leipzig.

It's really a very good job and it was very difficult to get. This week I had an interview with the director and convinced him that I was the one. The collective is very small, with only four co-workers and a secretary.

And it's only a five-minute walk from my apartment. What more could I want? It's very pleasant and the people have been very nice to me.

A new phase of my life is about to begin. I'm looking forward to this job very much – but with a little regret because the best time of my life – the university years – is perhaps now over. But other great times will certainly come! For sure!

Summer activities for Jürgen soon began: A paddleboat trip in June, and then the trip to Tashkent, Uzbekistan, and other parts of the Soviet Union.

Jürgen's comments on his new job conclude with a statement about the work ethic in the German Democratic Republic, and how proud he is of his country:

Yes – when I'm working I won't have so much vacation time, only four weeks a year. We Germans like to work too much! We are a hard-working people and are still the biggest and most beautiful GDR in the entire world. And so it will become even more beautiful. I'll work with everyone like it's expected. It's as simple as that.

(I did not write back to him to remind him that his country was the only GDR in the world.)

* * *

Gerhard's letter in May begins with this on my travel plans:

Your plans are just crazy! Oh, how I wish I could be there! How can you do it – each year traveling around the world? The Soviet Union doesn't really interest me much, but China does. That must be so very interesting, even though I know you're not going there now. When you're in the Soviet Union take just one more picture.

He also expresses an opinion on traveling in 1986 because of terrorist threats and the bombing of Libya, which President Reagan ordered, because two American soldiers had been killed in the bombing of a Berlin disco. Libyan terrorists had committed the attack.

You've certainly thought about the Arabs, but it appears you aren't worried. The whole thing makes me mad – the Arabs are apparently our friends. It's clear that it's just a band of murderers, and I can understand when the Americans feel they have to defend themselves. But it also shocked me when American bombs fell on Libya. One doesn't know if that's the end of it or the beginning of another war.

Life goes on for Gerhard, who filled me in on his vacation plans:

Everything is actually fine here. Since mid-May I've camped a lot with my tent, and naturally when the weather's nice I'm outside getting tan.

But I'm just not as enthusiastic about camping as I used to be. Things have changed a lot: You can't build a fire now, and people put a fence around their tent because they don't like to have contact with others.

I liked it better in Poland, but unfortunately the border is closed and won't be open very soon. How can the Poles look after the tourists when they have so little to eat themselves? It's really too bad.

What were, then, vacation possibilities, which, as we've seen, were very important to each of my East German friends? Gerhard continues:

> So, I've got to stay in the GDR – but at least I've got a place at the beach - that's what we call the Baltic here, because it's salty. But if there are just a few waves people aren't allowed to go swimming because again and again people drown in the small surf. But the waves aren't that high. But there are big waves in California! When I see pictures from your beaches, I then know what real waves are like!

Six years later Gerhard experienced the waves in California. He liked them.

His time on the Baltic coast ended after two weeks, and then he journeyed to the mountains, where exercise and hiking would let him "do something about my figure." After that, back to work he went because the summer would be over. And then:

> Life gets boring again. My motorcycle has to stay in the garage, my tent is stored. The only thing left is to look forward to next summer.

Gerhard also writes about the possibilities of building a house to live in with his girlfriend. But getting married won't happen soon:

> We don't want to get married because I have a big apartment, and many people get married just to get a bigger one.
>
> You can only build a house here when you have many children, otherwise you don't get permission to build.

In this letter Gerhard tells me about a situation he'd had with the police.

> Recently I had to go to court as a witness because I caught a purse-snatcher. He hit a woman and ran away with her purse. I was on my bike going to work and followed him, drove right between his legs with my bike [ouch!] and held him until the police came. He got ten months and a fine of 1500 marks.
>
> Normally I try not to have any contact with the police, but it's just not right when a man hits a woman and takes her purse.

In running his bike between the legs of the purse-snatcher, I think almost everyone can agree Gerhard did the right thing.

In May of 1986 there was increased tension on the border between West and East Berlin because East German border guards were demanding to see Western diplomats' passports instead of just their normal diplomatic passes. Gerhard tells what happened:

> You've certainly heard of the recent problems with the American Embassy here in East Berlin. I didn't want to go there while this was going on. I didn't want to get locked up

because of something stupid.

Then I heard it was impossible for an East Berliner even to go to the embassy. But I went anyway, checked out a couple of books and was asked for my ID papers upon leaving. But other than that, nothing happened. I even had my bag checked by embassy staff upon leaving, which usually doesn't happen.

But now all is back to normal, and I'm happy about that. I don't want to have to stop going to the embassy. It gives me that little feeling I'm in America. The people in the embassy are so friendly, and sometimes they even show movies.

It wouldn't be too long before Gerhard would experience the "real America." We just were not aware how quickly that opportunity would come.

Gerhard's concludes this letter with an interesting description of his everyday life. Quite normal, actually:

It's been quite hot here, and I've gone swimming a lot, but now it's raining, and I've got to close the window so that I don't freeze. But that's fine because when the weather is nice I'm always out and about and don't get anything done here at home.

But sometimes I've got to dust, wash clothes, and, as now, write letters. So everything has its good side. I've got to visit my girlfriend today, otherwise she'll be mad at me, and then I would have to look for a new one.

So – that's it for now. I'll sign off with the friendliest of greetings.

* * *

August was a busy travel month for Jürgen from Leipzig. An

extensive trip to Uzbekistan, a Soviet republic, ended with a day in Moscow.

My son and I were also in Uzbekistan that August, but our paths did not cross with Jürgen's. Rather than trying to write a narrative of his experiences and incorporating his quotes therein, I'd like to take a different approach. Jürgen's description is so thorough, that I'll quote it in its entirety so the reader can appreciate his very interesting travel experience:

Five weeks in Uzbekistan are over – and what remains are wonderful memories and plenty of photos.

We tried to find out what hotel you were in, but the Russian autocracy and the Uzbek easy way of doing things just made a joke out of trying to do this. It was simply impossible to get any information or to even leave a message at your hotel. We just gave up because every attempt fell flat.

We worked at a construction site with Czech and Hungarian students and naturally Uzbek construction workers. We didn't only work – we danced together, sang, drank green tea and the three weeks in Tashkent just flew by.

We got used to the food very quickly, even though it was almost always mutton.

The people were very nice and above all very curious because as Europeans we represented a kind of exoticism to them.

The students just asked a million questions. Some could barely distinguish between "Germany" and "German Democratic Republic," so we wound up teaching kind of a cultural course.

We particularly liked the old city of Tashkent and the bazaars.

Most impressive for me was our visit to the Martak-Chana madras, where students are educated in the Koran.

We visited a Muslim hour of prayer. When I look back at our five weeks there this was the most beautiful experience we had.

After three weeks in Tashkent we went to the Tienschan Mountains to relax. It was absolutely wonderful: The camp was on a reservoir with rugged cliffs and steep mountains on each side. We sunned ourselves for the first time in order to get a tan.

We were most heartily welcomed in a small mountain village where we were invited to tea, kefir, and goat cheese and had to taste fresh milk. Once again we experienced wonderful Uzbek hospitality, and we had to explain again about Europe. Comprehension was difficult because our hosts spoke no Russian, and we speak no Uzbek.

Buchara was **the** experience for me. The city enchanted me. It's like out of a fairy tale in *Thousand and One Nights*. We were very lucky to hear a concert by the Buchara Philharmonic played on traditional Uzbek instruments accompanied by the dancing of eight beautiful Uzbek ladies.

Three days in Samarkand weren't enough for us. We would have stayed longer had it been possible. But I have to be honest – after five weeks we were ready to get home and finally eat some European food and have an accompanying beer.

And finally, he concluded his vacation in Mecklenburg, an East German tourist region:

I was with friends canoeing in Mecklenburg. We were underway all day with two canoes, pitched our tents for the night and continued canoeing the next day. We did about twenty kilometers a day. That might not seem like much, but when one paddles all day into high waves and the wind is hitting you in the face one really knows in the evening how long 20 kilometers can be. But it's relaxing – we call it "active relaxation."

* * *

Barbara also had a very busy summer traveling. In her letter of October 19th she summarizes what turned out to be a very enjoyable summer. Travel was key – even though she still could not go to the West. I don't think it mattered.

Her bike trip from Mecklenburg to the Baltic:

Young people love to travel our small country from north to south and back – and it's really not very difficult. It's about one thousand kilometers. [That's over six hundred miles!]

In spite of bad weather – the low-pressure systems from Scotland and England always bring rain in the summer – it was a lot of fun, even silly, with great experiences of countryside and culture.

Barbara then traveled to Poland. In this letter is a very extensive summary of her experiences:

And then I went to a German summer course in southern Poland, on the border with Ukraine. I can hardly describe this country; I was so impressed with it that I didn't even want to go home after three weeks!

She spent three weeks with fellow Germans and Polish students of German – much like our summer program in Leipzig in 1983.

> There were a hundred students all crowded together in one student hotel so that encounters are inevitable, new ideas are presented and this led to clashes of different mentalities and cultures which took me to situations that I wasn't really used to.

> I've certainly become more aware and more connected with student life in Poland.

> Being a student there also means being well off and exclusive – more than in the GDR – so really nice activities, good conversations and true friendships are developed.

> After spending time with the students, we visited the wonderful city of Krakow for three days, where much from the middle ages has been preserved – churches, castles, towers, all abound. There are many sidewalk cafes in the city center. Gypsy bands make their way around, students sell pictures on the street, many galleries, boutiques, the old university, the Jewish quarter with cemetery and synagogues, flowers being sold everywhere – all of these things bring a super, super atmosphere to the old town. Even at night the streets are full of people.

Barbara also writes about Veit Stoß, a German Renaissance artist, many of whose carved wooden altars and religious statues eventually found their way to Poland. His Mary Altar was literally sawed off and taken to Nürnberg by the Nazis during the occupation of Poland. Through a "pirate action" (Barbara's words) after the war, a Polish professor got it back to Poland. "I had no idea how impressed I would be by its uniqueness and its balance of completely aesthetic configuration of figures."

A musical experience also presented itself. As she entered the courtyard of the castle of Wawel a choir from Warsaw was singing. Hearing the choir "was two or three times as nice in such surroundings."

"Krakow was really indescribable – it just lets itself be experienced."

Outdoor activities were not to be missed. On this same trip Barbara also hiked in the mountains of nearby Ukraine. "We slept in a farm in the hay, washed ourselves in the river – it was very romantic. For the first time I was able to see those crazy hang gliders."

Her letter continues with very interesting insight into Polish history and culture:

> In Lancet I saw for the first time a palace that was set up so visitors could see how people at one time actually lived there: bathroom, kitchen, library, ballroom, theater, and, and, and – everything as if it were just being used – all enclosed. Flowers and photos were in the rooms. The family lived here until 1945. It was one of the richest in Poland, and they were huge landowners in Ukraine – and went to the West with eleven train cars full of silver.

> The relationship of the Poles to their nobility is completely different than that in our country. The nobility is not the "evil feudal exploiters," but – since Poland was under Russian and czarist and other countries' domination, they are important historical figures of the nationalistic movement for Poland and therefore lauded by the people.

> The Poles have such a deep historical awareness, deal very

naturally with their background, their culture, their family (an important connection), with the still incredible connection with Catholicism.

Kids in jeans and "new fashion" didn't seem superficial at all. It just astonished me. Most of all, the hours I spent with the people in the hotel café were the best. It's a very nice arrangement: reading where newspapers from all over the world in all languages can be found.

The people have such a naturally free and enjoyable way of approaching life: proud of themselves, very individualistic, proud of their country and not so ostensibly didactic and morally judgmental as the Germans are.

What I'm saying concerns mainly the young people. The girls are to a certain great extent insecure and more timid like sheep, than we are. In addition, they seem to have an eye for the "superficial" things that make everyday life more fun: costume jewelry, flowers, ice cream, and cafes. I think this life style fits me more than that of the Germans. It was simply wonderful there.

Barbara did, however, get into political interaction with her Polish fellow students. This dealt with recent history – specifically the Solidarity Movement, of the early 1980s, led by Lech Walesa:

> Also interesting were naturally the discussions we had regarding Poland's most recent history: the uprisings in Danzig and Warsaw of the workers in 1981. This impulsive mentality differentiates the Poles from our German "theoretical" population.

As history would show, however, the East Germans became

less "theoretical" and more "impulsive" in the fall of 1989: *Die Wende* led to the opening of the Berlin Wall and a reunited Germany.

In typical "Barbara fashion," she concludes this letter with an apology I didn't find at all necessary:

> Please excuse that I've written this entire letter about myself and haven't asked at all about your trip to the Soviet Union. Maybe you could write me about your impressions, the atmosphere there, your evaluation.

* * *

This comment caused me to look back at that 1986 trip by re-reading more of my journal. Since the Soviet Union was the "mother country," so to speak, of the German Democratic Republic, the impressions and personal reactions I shared with Barbara could be interesting.

The Soviet Union was not a comfortable country. Our cab ride from the train station to the hotel in Moscow was "a wild ride over streets with big holes" where "pedestrians were expected to get out of the way." Television in the hotel was dominated by "commentary on Soviet peace initiatives, nuclear test ban initiatives, and attempts to halt the arms' race."

While traveling around Moscow I noticed "massive lines" of people trying to buy ice cream and drinking from "all use the same glass" soft drink dispensers. "The whole place has a GDR quality, maybe even a little worse, except for the massiveness of monuments."

Gregor Leonidovich, the gentleman I met from Kiev, was "absolutely certain all Intourist guides work for the KGB." (Intourist was the Soviet travel agency; the KGB was the state security service, much like the Stasi in East Germany.)

I was impressed by how busy people seemed to be: Lines everywhere, people walking, shopping, very crowded subway trains.

We then took the Trans-Siberian Express from Moscow to the Siberian city of Irkutsk, a four and a half day journey. Some observations from the train:

> Villages. Dirt streets, dirty rivers, serene scenes, kids swimming in ponds, people fishing, many obviously working in or walking through open fields.

Having traveled throughout much of East Germany, I wrote that the Soviet Union looked "poorer" and "much more basic" than the Democratic Republic. At night we passed through towns and train stations with hardly any lights on; even the larger cities weren't very well lit, when compared to a typical city in East Germany.

While our East Germans friends were very willing to share with us about their lives and country, it was different in the Soviet Union; our guide on the train said that she had been told, "to tell us not to take pictures of any bridges. Passengers are complaining of our group. Apparently foreigners aren't even allowed in the Urals."

The Urals are the mountain range that divides Europe from Asia in Russia. I'll never forget seeing the marker along the tracks that told us we had finally entered Asia.

My impression was that the people we saw from the train – I wondered if they should be called "peasants" - appeared to lead a "simple, hard life, carrying hand tools." Near a lumber mill there was "lots of broken stuff lying around." There were also very few private cars in the villages, towns and cities along the train route. This was great contrast to East Germany where traffic at times could be a problem, particularly in East Berlin, Leipzig and Dresden.

But modern times *had* arrived: "Most houses out here have TV antennas."

Another interesting sight was "ladies standing holding a yellow stick out to control traffic at each grade crossing."

No automatic train crossing signals in the middle of Siberia!

I was able to have a very interesting discussion one evening with the clerk in the hotel in Irkutsk. Her name was Vera. We talked until 2:00 am, and our discussion was not unlike those I'd had with East Germans. She asked, "Why Nicaragua, why homeless, why weapons?"

I asked her, "Why Afghanistan? Why barbed wire at the

border between Finland and the Soviet Union?" To which she replied the wire shouldn't be there – it's "one Earth." But the "borders are sealed to keep bad elements out."

I gave her a Beyond War pin and she seemed quite moved.

The last sentence in my journal entry for August 8, 1986 is: "Her driver, who heard our conversation, was also quite interested – Vera translated. I think I spread a little good will."

I'll conclude this "not about East Germany section" with an event on the train that I'll never forget: Three very cute little Russian girls – probably 5-8 years old – were playing in the corridor of our car. After an exchange of greetings, one of them looked at me and said: "Amerikanski, Russki . . . . Friend!"

Beautiful.

I eventually wrote back to Jürgen and told him about our trip. But apparently not soon enough. Well-deserved criticism was in a short note dated November 16th:

> Didn't you get my long letter about my experiences and my trip to the Soviet Union? Or have you just been too lazy to answer me? So, please sit down for an hour– I'm really interested and excited to learn about all the beautiful things you experienced in the summer! Please do me the favor! Please give me some notice that you're alive! Later.

Ouch.

* * *

Jutta expressed hopes for peace and less tension between

East and West in her letters of December. "Well," she asked. "Did you enjoy the meeting between Reagan and Gorbachev? I hope it means a real step forward towards security and further treaties."

I did. Maybe a relaxation of tensions was coming.

I had also sent her more materials from Beyond War, which she said were on their way to friends.

> I always admire the engagement of my American friends for peace and disarmament. We are so hermetically sealed off from the rest of the world that we can hardly dream of taking part in that peace movement as intensely, personally, and individually as you do over there. We are accustomed to act politically only by order, and only in that case are we obliged to act. Personal engagement is suspect, and for the "upper ones" it smells like betrayal. We have unlearned to act.

In December, Jutta also expressed frustration because I hadn't written since returning from our trip to the Soviet Union. "It's been a long time since you wrote me last. Nevertheless, I don't take it ill of you, as I guess you're quite a busy man! Let me know about your experiences."

Politics and hopes for a peaceful future concluded her wishes for 1987, but not without very directed criticism of President Reagan:

> Well, thinking of America presently means growing even madder at Ronnie's policy. It's hardly imaginable for a European citizen what's going on inside him. But one thing is

clear: No Western World boss is deeply interested in ending the arms' race.

* * *

However– as Barbara wrote in her Christmas greetings– hope for peace was not going to fade:

For 1987 I wish for all of us that the disarmament talks finally lead to actual results and that Reagan just doesn't keep up with his knee-jerk reactions! Get started with your Beyond War peace movement throughout the country!

Lots of love and all the best.

CHAPTER EIGHT

1987

Jürgen wrote the first letter I received in 1987. It was very short and contained an unnecessary apology: He hadn't been able to write to me because he had been in the army.

> Today I got your card from San Francisco – thank you very much! I also got your letter from January. [That was my letter to him reviewing my trip to the Soviet Union – finally!]
>
> The reason for my somewhat lengthy silence is really easy to explain: I was in the army for four months. And I had to, for various reasons, cut off my letter contacts with the USA – something I'm sure you can understand. But from today on everything's back to normal. I'm back at work and enjoying it very much.

* * *

1987 was the year in which at least some East Germans began to realize that change might be coming. There is evidence of this in a letter from Barbara written in June:

> Gorbachev's initiative to reorganize our society is still arousing and exciting all of us. Unfortunately, the shadows – as we Germans call it – of this development haven't yet stretched out towards the GDR. Our newspapers still overflow with self-

praise, records, superlatives.

Gorbachev grows into a person of importance for certainly all of us. There's rarely anyone who dislikes him. We all hope for the better his policy gives birth to.

I'd like to add something here. Today, as I write this, it is August 13, 2014. Exactly 53 years ago the East Germans began to build the Wall that was intended to permanently divide post-war Berlin. Thankfully, it lasted less than three decades.

My, how time flies!

* * *

In Jürgen's letter of September 17th I received another well-deserved reminder of my not writing as much as he would have liked. I did, however, appreciate his understanding my personal situation:

> You always want me to write to you – but how would it be if you could write something with a little more depth? You haven't written in a long time. You're certainly back to teaching. How are you doing?

> Your telling me that you were getting divorced shocked me. I hope you're doing fine and that all will come to a happy end. The world keeps turning – but what is it without love? I wish you all the best.

After vacationing in Poland– "there are just so many beautiful things to see" - and Prague, it was back to work at for

Jürgen at TransPress Publishing, where he'd received his first job after graduating from the university; he was also employed doing some free-lance work as a docent at the local equivalent of what Americans call "adult school." He taught two different German courses:

> The one course is made up of people from Poland; the other is more international, like what we had in Leipzig in '83. I've still got fond memories of that summer. In this course there are Poles, in addition to Russians, Cubans, Spaniards and Vietnamese. It really makes for a lot of fun. Perhaps I should have been a teacher?

Jürgen's teaching of an international German course also reminded me of the fine summer course I'd had in Leipzig four years earlier. It was good to read that the East Germans were still reaching out to German teachers from many countries; several North Koreans were also in our group. And I can say that there were no blatant attempts at "political indoctrination," even though the GDR was always spoken of and described in positive terms.

* * *

Barbara wrote in September a very informative letter about the lack of freedom she was experiencing. Because this is such an important topic, and she wrote so extensively, I think it's important to include my English translation of her entire letter:

It's now been half a year since I've tried to go to Moscow. I was so happy – an entire semester in another country, not as a tourist, but as someone really immersed in everyday life. It would have been beautiful!

As I was actually expecting the papers for the trip, I was told on the phone that my application had been denied. The reasons for denial are generally not given here. I was really shocked - not to be able to travel to the Soviet Union – God only knows – I never figured this would happen. One would only have thought that there would be no problem being able to travel to the Soviet Union. Since I was never told why, speculation ran rapid with me: Was there something in my papers that wasn't in order, was there a contingency question, were there reasons stemming from me as a person, from my biography, that worked against me?

At first I thought I was a "victim" of perestroika, the reform movement in the Soviet Union: Wider openness to the outside world, more opportunities to study, perhaps a reduction in funds because of some kind of graft activities. One just doesn't know.

And then I applied for permission to travel to West Berlin for my grandmother's 80th birthday. Perhaps you've heard that trips to West Germany, even the USA for relatives' anniversaries, weddings, or because of illness or funerals, have been handled quite liberally. That is, anybody who can show a true need to go to such things gets to go.

I'm of a different opinion. My local section supported this application and then it went to the administration of Karl Marx University - why I still don't know - that is, to people who would never know me, but would only have files or computer printouts on me. And I was denied! Does that mean there's something in my file? If so, what? And who knows something about that and where did they get the information?

These are all questions that make me very insecure and

mistrustful and questions to which I'll never get answers to in this country. This all makes me very unhappy. One explanation could be that some event in my life has branded me an "unreliable person" for sanctioned foreign travel. This just doesn't seem right.

She continues by saying that Chief of State Erich Honecker was in West Germany negotiating a loosening of travel restrictions and environmental, cultural, scientific, and technology agreements. The "shoot to kill" policy on the border was also to be lifted. And the East German flag was to be flown at official state visits, as well as the national anthem sung. But "the Federal Republic still doesn't, as before, recognize our citizenship and this has caused quite a stir." What appeared to be progress toward a relaxation of travel restrictions was not occurring, at least for Barbara. She summed up:

> One gets the impression this country is careening together into itself, the fundamental differences in status quo are becoming less distinct, and attempts are being made simply TO LIVE. But it's really quite easy to forget that the structures over which "big politics" hold sway, which are what really influence the lives of individuals, have not changed. It hurts a lot in the midst of all this euphoria to get smacked down, to be isolated from everyone, to find oneself suddenly again in the minority, which is in opposition to friends and acquaintances of both the right and the left, which these developments will hardly effect. And who knows how these friends and acquaintances will react to all of this?

An extremely interesting and informative characteristic of Barbara's letters was her descriptions of the countries that she did get permission to visit. In the summer of 1987 she went to Bulgaria, a "beautiful country, with beautiful cities and above all: SUN, SUN, SUN!!!" Getting out of the cold German "summer," as she put it, made her extremely happy. She experienced temperatures of 42 C, which would be about 106 F.

Apparently that wasn't too hot.

Sofia, Bulgaria, was just remarkable: Turkish and ancient Roman architecture, but at the same time, entirely modern.

> Many cafes and small parks that really make one want to just stroll. Lots of really colorful people. Life on the streets until 10:00 at night: drinking coffee, nibbling on fruit, eating ice cream, and watching, watching, watching. . . Just wonderful – not at all Germanic. In our country everything just seems to creep so quickly within itself into our four walls – too bad.

However, Bulgaria did not escape criticism. Barbara was disturbed by what she called "Prussianism in the Balkans":

> Uniforms are very important and accordingly play quite a big role in society. Also, even though we were dealt with in nearly all cases in a very pleasant way, there's a certain haughtiness that's based on shallow arrogance, that can't be avoided, particularly among the overdressed young men.

Barbara also had the opportunity to observe some aspects of Bulgarian society: "The social differences among gypsies, farmers, and city folk are very distinct. Society is much more hierarchically structured than in our country, where a socially broad majority dominates."

The highpoint of her vacation in Bulgaria was a week in the mountains of Rhodopen.

> We went with tents and heavy backpacks from the south, near the Greek border, north to the monastery at Batschkovo. We were really taken into nature: water from cold mountain springs, tents, soup and divided-up rations of bread. We had to carry everything on our backs and we had no re-supply. On top of all this was the physical exertion, even though it was only a mid-level mountain range it had steep ups and downs and paths that were not well marked. When we finally got to our destination we all had knee, toe and hip pain, and were completely exhausted. But no one would have traded this romantic adventure and accomplishment for anything.

All vacations end, though. Having gotten permission from the authorities, Barbara and Andreas started building their house in Löwendorf, a small village near Berlin, in August. It was stressful, but there weren't really any problems.

> The physical work was really fun: lugging rocks, mixing concrete, digging foundations and pouring them, trimming packing material, tarring the insulation on the outside of the cellar. I learned a lot while doing all of this. Since we had time, Andreas and I did a lot by ourselves. However, being alone in this village caused emptiness in me. I need hustle and bustle and my friends, a change of pace...

* * *

I wrote to Jürgen in October, and he commented: "Finally I got a letter from you – I, too, don't like to write long detailed letters in the summer."

I guess I hadn't written a really long and detailed letter.

But he did, telling me about working with Poles, his opinions on Cubans, 1987's Nobel Prizes for literature and peace, and Gorbachev's contributions to the relaxation of tensions between East and West.

Poland:

> This is a country where people are nice and the youth are much more serious than the Germans. They're willing to talk about anything. I'm always impressed by the Poles' beliefs. Almost everyone is Catholic. If one respects their beliefs, many opportunities for genuine discussions present themselves. They are so full of culture and know a lot about music and they certainly read as much as the Germans. The young men are particularly open – and the women are known for their beauty.

He also had the opportunity to work with Cuban students in the evening adult education school where he taught for a while. He was quite critical:

> And then there are the Cubans, whom I find difficult to work with. They are very undisciplined, speak loudly during instruction, are impatient, and when a classmate doesn't know the answer, they answer for him. They seem so uncultured. One can hardly hold a conversation with them about literature. They hardly know an author. Sometimes it's really bad.

I learned a lot about Jürgen's opinions on world peace through his comments on the Nobel Prize for Literature and Mr. Gorbachev. He was very disappointed in who won the prize, the

Russian author Joseph Brodsky.

> I found it very undiplomatic to give the prize this year to a Russian who left his country and was such a critic of the Soviet system. And that's in a year when Gorbachev has contributed so much to the relaxation of tensions. The hardening of positions between the two sides had become more normal. Both parties now sit at the negotiating table. That is really success! And then a man is honored in Stockholm who has developed himself into a true anti-communist and anti-Soviet.
>
> I don't know, but sometimes I think that we just live in a really screwed up world. In the USA people most certainly must have been happy. But in my opinion, it's a blow to all those who are trying to make a more peaceful world. Disappointment just spreads.
>
> Otherwise life goes on. We just need to make the best of it. So, my dear friend, that's it for today. I hope I've been able to divert you a little.

To complete 1987's correspondence, Jürgen wishes me a Merry Christmas and briefly describes the Holiday season in Leipzig:

> Here the Christmas festival is really more a time of reflection, a quiet festival, but something that demands a lot of time and effort. We'll celebrate quietly until New Year's. I wish you all the best for 1988!

He concludes with an expression of hope for improved international relations:

> Let's hope that the summit meetings in Washington between

President Reagan and General Secretary Gorbachev bear a lot of fruit, and that the relations between countries continue to improve.

Relations were about to improve; there were only two more years until November 1989.

* * *

A long letter from Barbara arrived during Christmas break of 1987. I'd finally written to her, and she seemed to appreciate our writing to each other:

> I really enjoyed all the mail you recently sent me— a card from your vacation, your long letter and the Christmas greeting all arrived. It's good to be in contact with someone on the other side of the Atlantic. Your reports of your daily activities and the films and newspapers from the USA are something special each time they all get here. I envy you with your excursions and journeys. Oh well, another world…

However, things with Andreas weren't working out, and this was making life more difficult for her. She's 25 years old and in two years will be getting her degree from the University of Leipzig. She is trying to give her life "some appropriate direction, not the least of which is to find a job," writing in detail about her situation:

> The biggest problem at this time is between Andreas and me. It is that he would like for me to become really close to his parents, and this house that we're building and this village.

I'm happy with my own family and my private activities.

It's also become slowly clearer to me that an overwhelming amount of circumstances is coming together, and I'm finding that I have to combat more than idealism. And that doesn't have to be.

Housework and garden are not really all that I want in life. What would be wrong with a small apartment in Berlin? But Andreas isn't going along with this. The house, the village, his family are what's really important.

But that's not all: he wants to make jewelry and pottery when he completes his last voyage at sea. And that can only happen in our village. But I have to be among many people who have the same interests as I do, in an intellectual sense, and be surrounded with literature.

Making decisions is just crazily difficult – how often does one just let time work for oneself, as well as just reflecting about things that are controversial?

And the other thing is living with the consequences of one's actions. There just aren't any clear, "clean" solutions. There's always some kind of unpleasantness left over. And that makes life more difficult. Not being afraid of changes, and letting things just happen, is something that I have to always tell myself to keep in mind.

Finally this one life that we have just needs to take its most optimal course. Ingeborg Bachmann (an Austrian author!!) has wondered if, through the constant conquering of borders (one's own borders and those imposed from outside), a sense of life can exist at all. I think there's a lot in what she says. And after contemplating this a lot, one has the feeling that it doesn't help to keep all of this in front of us.

Oh well, beating one's self up with this doesn't help at all. We'll just have to see.

Barbara then expresses hope for our being able to see each other again, possibly in Berlin, the following summer. But not, unfortunately, in California: "It would be just so great if we could get together! I just can't imagine a trip to California." After this sentence she drew a cute, winking happy face. "But it would just cost so much for such a trip – at least seven dollars! Ridiculous!"

Yes– even East Germans had a great sense of humor.

She continued by expressing more frustration with travel restrictions:

I know people who have flown to the USA to visit brothers or sisters, among others, but my application to visit my 80-year-old grandmother in West Berlin in October for a week was denied by the university. It didn't even get to the public authorities. I was very very angry and beaten down, because one can't do anything other than try again and again, just to see if somehow one can be successful with such an attempt.

Meanwhile what is so certain for so many– the permission to travel– and how they succeed, I just don't get it. It's very unsettling.

In less than two years– in November of 1989– Barbara would be able to travel anywhere she wants.

Prospects for peace also began to improve. The Reagan-Gorbachev summit in Washington was giving East Germans hope for the future. Barbara wrote:

I'm really happy that it looks like something will come out of the summit. An entire class of weapons could disappear. Unimaginable! But trepidation is still there and is so strong because the threat has not really been reduced. There are still so many weapons!

But Barbara is not too sure what the future holds.

Is this all leading to "a new way of thinking?" she asks. (I found it very interesting that she quoted in English our Beyond War motto.) "Could this be our only chance?" she also asks.

Why is there no profit-motivated disarmament industry? It can't be as unproductive as the armaments' industry, can it? It's the super powers that are negotiating now. Who's paying attention to the other countries: Israel, France, China, and the states of the Persian Gulf? This joy cannot help the weaker states.

Barbara concludes this letter, written on December 21st, with Christmas greetings that were so typical of the sincere wishes I got each year from my East German friends:

Dear David, I wish you all the very best at Christmas and for the New Year: Peace, many beautiful experiences, and journeys (to the GDR!), and that all things possible for you come to fruition.

David F. Strack

CHAPTER NINE

1988

By 1988 the East German regime continued to loosen travel restrictions. In January I received a letter from Jutta that contained some wonderful news:

> In the meantime I visited Western Germany. It was a really thrilling happening – to cross the Iron Curtain, and as I stepped onto the Frankfurt ground my knees went soft. After some further steps I began to weep, as a result of my confused emotions and nerves. It's beyond description; no one can fancy that but my own experience of being captured in a cage.

A major problem with such travel for an East German was money that could be used in the West. The East Mark had no value outside of the Democratic Republic; it wasn't even accepted at currency exchanges. She therefore had to somehow get West marks – or even U.S. dollars – in order to cover her expenses while traveling in the Federal Republic. This would also be the case for "other spots in Europe (or even America!?!)."

But how was this to happen? Jutta was open and honest:

> I urgently need more money. Dear David, will you please help

me? The question is not to get *much*, but to get *some* money *at all*. Please don't take it bad. I do not want to become rich or to buy desired articles. My idea is of quite an "idealist" nature: to see a bit more of this multicolored world, which so far was quite a hidden empire for me throughout many, many years. This dream is realizable but by money.

I understood completely what she was saying. East Germans just didn't have the funds then to travel out of the country, once such travel was permitted.

Jutta received enough money so she could travel.

Her first trip to West Germany was "very stirring, filled with meetings with new people, sleepless nights, mixed emotions. I lived with several families mostly of middle class."

Her travels to the Federal Republic continued; after unification in 1990, she even traveled to Australia for study and to translate Australian literature into German. In 1998 her "dream trip," as she put it, took place when she and her two sons traveled to California.

* * *

Leipzig was the book-publishing center for East Germany. Every spring the Leipzig Trade Show included the country's largest book exhibition. Jürgen, as we've read, worked for a publishing house, and was therefore able to see first-hand what books were available internationally: "That's always for us a special experience, because we also produce books in our publishing house and therefore can compare our books with those on the international market."

Many books published in the USA were on display at the book fair. These books impressed him, particularly from a design standpoint:

> The USA books distinguish themselves through first class printing techniques and wonderful colors. But the books from the GDR are also quite good. If we only didn't have this exasperating problem of paper production. Our production rises and falls with that.

And what about the purchasing of these USA-published books in the GDR? "One can't buy these books here. If that were to happen, there would be such a great demand that it just couldn't be satisfied."

$$* * *$$

Barbara continues to write about getting her degree that spring, having just presented the first chapter of her dissertation before the faculty committee.

> It really tortured me, but in the end it went quite well, and I was able for the most part to calm my nerves. But I was really able to handle the whole thing and not to let myself be beat up by the situation. Now I can calmly march into summer.

Summer meant more travel plans, restricted as they may have been: A trip to the northern coast to the cities of Rostock and

Wismar where she can get out of the "wasteland" of Leipzig, as she called it. She could then enjoy an area where "spring really takes place and we can gather strength for the less enjoyable stuff" that lay ahead: "Our house must be built by May/June. Oh, well."

East Germans were not kept from traveling east. In March Barbara had been with her brother in Budapest, Hungary. Her comments regarding this important East Bloc country are quite informative as are her opinions of an economy that was gradually becoming westernized:

> It was somewhat perplexing for me. Everything in this country seems to be ruled by "money." Everything revolves around it. For some it's because they've always got to consider where the money is coming from in order to be able to live as they imagine they can – having a profession now just doesn't cut it.
>
> For others it's because they've obtained such oodles of money that it's just become their purpose in life. It seems there's everything there, a lot from the West, but the prices are enormously high and inflation just keeps going up. People have gone in the last few years maybe a bit too far in their desire to achieve a free market economy. The stress that comes out of all this is terrible for some. Superficially it looks as if it could be the country we could look to as the best place – but there is just so little appeal.

By January of 1988 Czechoslovakia had opened its borders, due to the reforms instituted by Vaclav Havel. Barbara writes many Czechoslovaks were able to go "anywhere they want. And that makes for very attractive advantages. But for us only

Hungary is possible."

There had also been a reduction in the amount of money East Germans could exchange: thirty marks per day, and totally only enough for twelve days a year. This did not make her happy:

> Ridiculous! That won't even cover room and board for half that amount of time! One alternative: go with an organized tour booked through a travel agency. And now I'm a great friend of *that*! Makes me crazy! One just can't even think about it!

1988 was, however, bringing some hope for significant change:

> Things here are getting a little more liberalized and realistic. But it's still quite confusing, because we don't know where everything is headed, if things will develop in one direction or another– demonstrations and arrests, people leaving the country.
>
> There's conflict between state and the church as an autonomous institution, which will also bring a lot of political opposition. All in all, one doesn't notice much of this in one's everyday life. In the winter things got rather tense. Some of our leaders were expelled to West Germany, so that now everything is a bit calmer. People are becoming more self-confident here, and that is very good and pleasant.
>
> The injustices are getting people more agitated. What Gorbachev is doing is having an effect here. Perhaps, perhaps, we'll experience change for the better. Take a look this summer and see what you think if things look different. We'll see each other on 30 June. I'm really looking forward to it!

June 30, 1988 finally arrived. We – some students, friends of mine, and I – spent several hours in East Berlin with Jürgen, Barbara, their friend Walter, and Astryd, a German teacher from Norway, whom I'd met in Leipzig in 1983. We all met at the Friedrichstrasse station, the main crossing point for Westerners to get into East Berlin.

It was a fine day: We walked through the restored Nikolai Quarter, took the S-Bahn to the suburb of Körpenick and had lunch there in the Ratskeller, the city hall restaurant. The rest of the afternoon we walked, saw various sites, and enjoyed each other's company. At 5:00 in the afternoon we said our good-byes, and my students and I re-entered West Berlin.

The main crossing site back into West Berlin then had an interesting nickname in German: *Palast der Tränen* - "Palace of Tears." (The sign saying this was only visible from West Berlin.) What Barbara and Jürgen wrote after our day together in East Berlin gave credence as to why this building was called "Palace of Tears."

Jürgen:

It was so beautiful seeing you again, but unfortunately the time just went by so fast. And the sad departure of you guys at the border just about did us all in. First of all, we just walked aimlessly along the Spree [Berlin's river] until we could find the words to talk.

We went to a café and spent all the money we got from you. We drank to the quick disappearance of the Wall so that we can visit each other where we want. We drank to German-American friendship and to our friends. Please visit us again soon– as long as we can't visit you!

Barbara:

And just a couple of days ago you were in Berlin. It's so strange that it's been five years since we met, but it was really so normal that it seems like only weeks passed until we met again. You were not at all foreign, and just as I had imagined you to be, just like I remembered you.

I was very curious about the day and was so happy to have seen you again. Saying good-bye at the border, oh, well. . . It would have been so normal for all of us to go in the evening to a disco. . . So we took our "Weltschmerz" and the East marks you gave us to a nearby, very nice café. I've enclosed the "bill" so that you know we used the money wisely: champagne, schnapps, and coffee. . . It was a great way to end the day.

But life went on and vacations were taken. Camping was a very important way for East Germans to connect with nature. Barbara writes on July 17th, while camping in the lake district of northern Germany, that many kilometers were covered canoeing each day on lakes and rivers:

In the last few years I'd always been in a foreign country on vacation and didn't think our tiny country had anything as beautiful as this – everything is so green and it all leads to a soft landscape with sleepy villages.

She and her friends camped after many hours each day of rowing where "trees hung a great deal over the water and the lily pads bloomed on our oars." She wrote this in her tent that evening:

> My friends have just called to me, asking me what I've been doing for so long, if I'm secretly writing poems, or if I've already gone to sleep. . . A letter to David, aha! Now I'm supposed to greet you from all of them— even though they don't know you. Great— that, too! And if I don't come right now all of the wine will be gone! So— I can't compete with that and now will conclude this letter. The dearest of greetings and come back again!

I did go back. The next time I saw Barbara, Jürgen and Gerhard would be in December of 1989, six weeks after the opening of the Wall.

In July of 1988 none of us had any idea it would come so soon.

* * *

During that summer of 1988, Jutta wrote that she experienced some important changes in her profession of translating. In April, she gave notice to her publishing house that she was no longer going to work there. She had moved on to "doing this and that, without a work contract. The major task for me now consists of translating English literature into German for Reclam publishing house." Her other translating work included Canadian Inuit legends into German and a German fashion monthly into English that was then exported to Syria and India.

I don't know why the hell East German fashion is worthwhile there!! And I'm also teaching English to a class of advanced students at a foreign trade technical school. So I'm occupied with several doings and feeling well about it.

* * *

In 1988, American movies and literature were finally not banned in the German Democratic Republic. Barbara enclosed a critique of a Steven Spielberg movie from a GDR movie journal: *E.T.* was playing and "attracting thousands of viewers." And *The Color Purple* would be playing soon. She was also reading Sinclair Lewis' *It Can't Happen Here*. Next on her reading list was *The World According to Garp*, by John Irving.

And examinations loomed:

> At the end of June I'll have to cope with my first exams for becoming a translator/interpreter. This will enable me to officially have a second profession, which fortunately makes me more independent than that of being a Germanist, where my degree basically just allows me to teach German.

* * *

Jutta also mentions that since travel between the two Germanys had become less restrictive, she was looking forward to friends, whom she had met on her visit to West Germany the previous autumn, coming to Leipzig.

> The young people there took a deep interest in our way of life here, and we had an intense exchange of ideas and opinions. I

hope to show them a whole lot of Leipzig and its surroundings, and that they'll meet some friends of mine.

* * *

Barbara and Andreas got married in August! She wrote that they were able to work through the situation that was making problems for them earlier in their relationship: Andreas wanted to live in a small village near his parents, she saw herself as a "city person." They even considered a separation:

> But that would have led to a "no" to getting married. Perhaps in another country we could have just lived together, but the GDR wouldn't have it any other way. It's because of travel – Andreas could take me along when we have this stamp on our passports. We'd love each other even without this paper! He will still go to sea, the house will be built, and I'll take the position at the Academy of the Arts and get a room in Berlin. Very complicated, but we want to do it.

Barbara describes their wedding day:

> We got married completely alone and unconventionally at a beach resort. It was a beautiful day: We took an early walk on the beach on the promenade and in the water. Only because of our bouquet of roses with the white ribbon could anyone tell what was going on. People were really happy when they saw us; many strangers came and congratulated us on the way to the beach. It was fun.

> Then we visited the cathedral in Bad Doberan and finally had fried eggs and bacon for lunch at a place for truckers on the highway. That was fun. The waiter was something else! We hadn't planned anything and just let everything develop by chance.

In the afternoon we were in Warnemünde on the promenade, the breakwater, and the flea market. In the evening we ate Chinese in a small salon in a hotel in Rostock and ended our stroll along the coast. We had wonderful summer weather and got really silly. Afterwards we were twice as happy because of all the relatives who showed up and helped us realize our plans... Andreas' father kind of complained because he thought he was being bilked out of some money. My parents said we did the event just right because we made the day so beautiful for ourselves... Oh well, to do right for everyone is an art that no one can really do.

The topic in this letter then turns to travel with Barbara writing, that while travel is something she and Andreas like to do, they actually prefer hiking. They would like to visit the Soviet Union, but it's very difficult for them as tourists unless they were to join a group tour. But: "We really don't like these booked and planned tours."

Unfortunately, GDR citizens were still facing numerous travel restrictions.

I had already told her that I was planning another trip to the Soviet Union in the summer of 1989. Her comment: "I think it's great that you come back again and again to Germany and are looking at going to the Soviet Union again."

She continues commenting on the current political situations:

There are certainly many prejudices in the USA that we don't have here or in the Soviet Union. That you don't let yourself be impressed by such things and are honestly interested I find, not only from private reasons good, but also entirely human.

Confronting oneself as human and not accepting the irrelevant "rules of the game" of the greater political system is truly a new way to live.

Barbara even writes about the 1988 American presidential campaign. She has a definite opinion: "Jesse Jackson would have been for me the best presidential candidate, because his demands really are orientated to the people."

She concludes this letter with a very interesting statement regarding economics, the Cold War, and the environment. It's an example of how concerned East Germans were with these issues in the 1980s:

The politics of today seem to be distancing themselves from the people, be it through consumerism, weapons or through ignoring of needs of the environment. But something more intelligent I just personally don't see happening: stopping the use of spray bottles, recycling, putting living ahead of material things and relations that stretch over borders.

* * *

In her letter of October 10th, Jutta writes about her second trip to West Germany. She stayed in Eltville, a pleasant town on the Rhein, with our friend Linda (who was in the 1974 group that first met Gerhard) and her husband, Stefan. Linda at that time was teaching German at the U.S. forces' base in Wiesbaden. Jutta enjoyed "participating in Linda's German class, talking with the Americans there." She had a very interesting trip, meeting new people and visiting other towns:

> This time, I wasn't that excited and as overwhelmed as I was last year: I took all experiences, talks, and happenings more calmly and restfully. Now I've come to experience West Germany as naturally as anyone else who gets to travel.

Jutta's living situation had changed for the better. Her daughter, Judith, was in the 2nd grade, her son David in pre-school. They now live in a four-room apartment that was "quite satisfying after having spent several years as four people in a two room flat. The conditions of reading, studying, working, having guests and friends are really enjoyable."

However, travel was not yet a family activity. Andreas, her husband, in his third year of medical school, still was not allowed to travel to the West. "Andreas has no opportunity to cross the border. It's just me who has an uncle 'over there.' "

This was the first time I'd read or heard that Jutta had an uncle in the West. I can only assume he did exist…

David F. Strack

CHAPTER TEN

1989

The year of *Die Wende* — the "turn" or "change in direction"— finally arrived. (Remember, this word was used by Barbara back in 1986.) Things were changing in the German Democratic Republic, and the letters I received from Jürgen, Barbara, and Gerhard before November 9th, contained both hope and doubt.

* * *

Let's start with Jürgen. In March he was very busy working for the publishing house:

> I'm working at home on the first pages of our catalogue, putting the pictures together with the appropriate pages and titles and sub-titles. It's a lot of fun and it enables me to earn more money.

> I'm also teaching at the adult school, but it's a real challenge because both groups are true beginners and don't speak a word of German. So I talk twice a week for 90 minutes uninterrupted, in addition to hours of preparation and the grading of papers.

And typical German bureaucracy also has to be dealt with:

There are also all the formalities: lists, forms, ID papers and other papers that the Germans love so much.

Oh well, time just goes by.

You seem really occupied with the Berlin Wall. But what can I say? You've seen for yourself how sad it is when you guys disappear behind it. Even worse is having to stay on this side. Remember how I wrote you that Walter, Barbara and I sat in that café and hardly were able to speak?

Then he expresses doubt as to whether the Wall would ever come down. Referring to General Secretary Mikhail Gorbachev's policy of *glasnost*, which was the new Soviet policy of increased openness and transparency in government, institutions and activities, Jürgen wrote this:

If *glasnost* will change anything soon I really doubt. A couple of weeks ago Honecker [East Germany's Communist Party chief] said the Wall will still be standing in *fifty or one hundred years* if the political situation in Europe doesn't change accordingly. What can one say to that? Sometimes I don't even know what I'm supposed to think. I don't believe that we'll ever experience the falling of the Wall. Even though *glasnost* has given us some hope. But not necessarily related just to the Wall, but in general. People don't really want to concern themselves with this subject here. "When your neighbor renovates his place it doesn't mean that we have to install new carpeting." Those are the words of our chief ideologue.

Think about that a little bit.

During these years the Soviet Union published a German language magazine, *Sputnik*. Jürgen writes that it had just been forbidden in the GDR, "ostensibly because of falsification of historical facts, as well as misrepresentation of history."

I think it's another example of the GDR regime trying to hold on to power, realizing that in 1989 the people were beginning to demand significant change. *Neues Deutschland*, the Communist Party newspaper, was the official state publication that gave people the information deemed necessary. But apparently *Sputnik* was publishing historical facts that the East German Communist Party felt should not be learned by the population in general.

Quoting Jürgen:

The Stalin years: "Much was just recently written in *Sputnik* about the Stalin times that was quite interesting because this chapter of history is not taught in our schools." (He doesn't mention what was "quite interesting" of the Stalin times that was not taught in GDR schools. My guess is that it was the purges of the late 1930s when millions were executed.)

Leonid Brezhnev: "The Brezhnev era is also being held to account now. That's worthwhile now because we haven't taken that step here yet."

Afghanistan: "And last, but not least, an evaluation of the Afghanistan conflict."

These statements give us an indication of the effect of

glasnost, and how Mr. Gorbachev's policies were changing the Soviet Union and were about to bring significant change in the Soviet satellite countries.

Jürgen, in his letter written on March 5, 1989, expressed his desire for change, something he had not actually done earlier:

> Unfortunately, it's really only possible to get such information from Western TV. Too bad, too bad. You can see we really have a need here to catch up with events. Maybe some things will at least begin to change here a little.

But he still had to deal with travel restrictions. I had told him I would be in the Soviet Union with my daughter, Allison, and a group of students and adults that coming summer. He wrote again expressing frustration with the travel rights of East Germans:

> But still something about your trip to the Soviet Union. That's just great for you and hopefully for your daughter. But there's no way I'll be able to get to Moscow. I'm sorry, but that just isn't going to happen. One can only go with travel groups, and because of that one just can't have private meetings with others.

In June Jürgen took a "hiking vacation," which seemed so typical for many East Germans. He and six friends hiked 120 kilometers in six days on a path that went through the Thuringer forest. Every day they hiked twenty kilometers carrying backpacks that weighed over forty pounds.

I've seldom been so happy with a vacation: Six to seven hours per day, always in beautiful forests, in fresh air. Elevations of between 700 and 950 meters [approximately 2000` to 3000`]; wonderfully quiet. Only in the villages and small towns did we meet a few other people. We were just surrounded by nature.

But, as always, the trip was just too short.

However, the political situation and the Wall did not escape being mentioned, even after a wonderful vacation. He summarized an article that had been in the Leipzig newspapers:

The article is about U.S. soldiers who are stationed in West Berlin, and every week they take shopping trips to East Berlin. Since I've been often in Berlin, I've also experienced this: Soldiers with gigantic packages of toys, children's clothing, etc. They spend 500 to 700 marks in one day, that is, for comparison's sake, an entire month's salary for me. But with the exchange rate the Americans get, they can afford to do such a thing. And the Wall doesn't help because the Americans are treated like diplomats. Exactly this situation led to the construction of the Wall, as plundering took over because of such favorable exchange rates everything was simply sold out. You see– it's still going on!

Little did I know that things were about to change more rapidly in Germany than I had ever imagined. People would ask me: "David, when do you think the Wall will come down?" My response was always something like this: "Probably not in our lifetimes."

* * *

But in July of 1989 – four months before the opening of the Wall - Gerhard got permission to travel to West Berlin! What a complete and joyful surprise! Things were changing so rapidly that summer in East Germany; Gerhard's being able to get to West Berlin was just one example. Here's what he wrote in August:

> I've moved again and now live in West Berlin. It really wasn't all as dramatic as you might imagine. My cousin, who lives in West Berlin, invited me to his 65th birthday celebration. To my great surprise I got a passport and was able to travel.
>
> The next day I applied for refugee status in the West and since then I'm living in a refugee camp. The formalities are all taken care of. I've also got a job and am looking for an apartment. That appears to be a problem. But once I have it I'm really starting over with nothing. I've got to buy everything because I couldn't bring anything with me.
>
> In a year I should be ok and then be able to dedicate myself to what my true hobby is: travel. I'm really looking forward to visiting California! But I can't go back to East Berlin for about seven years because I've been sentenced to two years of prison in absentia. I've got to wait for amnesty. Bad, right?

Skipping ahead a bit, I'd like to add here a brief summary of his California trip. In March of 1991 he visited me, finally able to pursue his "hobby" of travel: San Diego, Tijuana, Mexico, Arizona, Grand Canyon, the Colorado River and many points in between.

I was his driver.

The highlight of the trip was our time at the Grand Canyon. I'll never forget that when we stood on the rim of that beautiful place, tears came to his eyes.

Gerhard was free.

But now back to 1989. Throughout this year it was becoming obvious that East Germany was on the threshold of great change: there were fewer travel restrictions. The border with Hungary was opened, so those East Germans who could get to Hungary could board a train and travel to West Germany.

Demonstrations for more freedoms were taking place in cities such as Leipzig and East Berlin.

* * *

On October 28, 1989, just weeks before the opening of the Berlin Wall, Jutta wrote a letter in which she describes how things were building to *Die Wende*:

> Much is in the air here in the GDR: We are torn between hope and skepticism. Our Chief is responsible for many crimes of the past – brutal police terror during the demonstrations, elections' deceit in May.
>
> We want power to be shared with the admission of opposition parties and unions, a new constitution, the end of all privileges, new elections, an educational system free of ideological influences, public control of all and everything, media, statistics, law, departments, housing admissions, ecology etc., etc.
>
> What has definitely changed is the content of our papers,

which turned into a most interesting media of reports and readers' opinions.

Yesterday an amnesty of all who left the GDR illegally, and of those who tried, but failed, took place. And moreover, the border to Czechoslovakia will be opened again. These are the first real results of a change, or WENDE, as we call it.

We are all stirred, touched at our innermost, strained and stressed by will, hope, skepticism, and longing for a future worth living. We long for possibilities to travel around freely. A travel law will be discussed in parliament soon. We don't dare fancy open borders, being free and easy.

Keep your fingers crossed for us! We are a desperate people – up to now. Delivered to the mercies of the same people who have forever reigned here in the GDR.

CHAPTER ELEVEN
November 9, 1989

We *did* keep our fingers crossed. And it happened. The Wall was opened at around midnight, Berlin time.

I remember ever so clearly when I learned that it had happened: I taught my regular classes at Yucaipa High School and was not aware of the events that had taken place in Berlin earlier that day.

It was a cool and sunny Southern California fall afternoon. I had to home-teach a student because of her impending surgery. I arrived at her house at 4:00 pm. Allison answered the door and the first thing she said to me was: "Mr. Strack did you hear? They've opened the Berlin Wall!" It is one of those moments one does not forget.

The German lesson was given, and home I went – to non-stop news coverage of what was happening in Berlin.

It wasn't long before I realized that I *had* to get to Berlin. My good friend Ivan and I soon made plans.

We arrived in Berlin on December 18th, returning home on the 24th. We picked this time frame so we could experience the opening of the Brandenburg Gate to east-west foot traffic on

December 22nd.

We would also be able to see three of our East German friends: Jürgen and Barbara from Leipzig, and Gerhard, from Berlin; we'd been corresponding since 1974. He was in West Berlin now – so, no problem!

Jutta was just not able to get to Berlin during the time we would be there.

* * *

Jürgen seemed to be looking forward to seeing us:

Man – what a surprise! Your letter made me really happy, and even more so since we're going to be seeing each other in Berlin. I've also spoken with Barbara. We both want to come to Berlin on Tuesday and pick you guys up at the train. We'll let Gerhard know what's going on.

Yes, unbelievable change was taking place.

Jürgen, who over the years seemed quite supportive of the socialist system and critical of many things in the West, concluded his short letter with this:

"So – until Tuesday! Hearty greetings from the City of Heroes!"

Die Wende had arrived. And it had begun in Leipzig – the City of Heroes.

CHAPTER TWELVE
December 19-22, 1989

We all were able to get together in both West *and* East Berlin. The highlight of our time in Berlin was the re-opening of the Brandenburg gate on that rainy evening of December 22nd.

Jürgen and Barbara met us at the Berlin train station. We called Gerhard, and then we all went to his apartment for coffee. The discussion centered around their telling us about what it was like to be in Berlin when the Wall opened up on November 9th. They all couldn't believe it was happening.

But it was– and they were free.

One of the first things we had to do was get our own pieces of the Wall. We were about to become "Wall Peckers," the term the Germans used for people who were chipping away at the Wall. Gerhard brought gloves, hammers and chisels and off we went. We chipped and chiseled not too far from the Brandenburg Gate. It was simply unbelievable that this was happening! Dozens of Wall Peckers were busy, getting their pieces of the west side of the Berlin Wall; that was the side to chip away at, because the eastern side had no graffiti, no slogans, no "art." Gerhard even brought us a snack of sausages and "Glühwein," a warm, sweetened red wine that Germans drink as a traditional Christmas beverage.

After an hour or so, I knew I'd had as many pieces as I needed: Family and friends would receive a piece of the Wall; as a surprise for my students at Yucaipa High School, each would get a little souvenir from Berlin.

With color, of course.

We then walked to one of the crossing points that had been opened at Potsdammer Platz. It was truly an incredible scene: East German border guards walking into the West, chatting with tourists and West Berlin police; they were even taking pictures. "How's this all going to work out?" was the question we asked our friends. Jürgen and Barbara both agreed it was too early to tell – but "there's no going back now."

On the next day we went to East Berlin again, this time through Checkpoint Charlie, the main border crossing for Americans. But Gerhard, being a German, could not cross there. The guards were very friendly and helpful: he'd have to go to Potsdammer Platz. No problem. Thirty minutes later we were together again and went to visit the site of the Potsdam Conference where in 1945 Truman, Stalin and Churchill decided how a defeated Germany would finally be occupied.

This day concluded with a visit to Gerhard's mother's house, where we also met his brother. The conversation naturally was centered on what was happening in East Germany.

"Unbelievable that all of this has happened in such a short period of time." The Stasi – state security service – had been removed from their neighborhood. All of them had already been to West Berlin and were overwhelmed by the courtesy and friendliness of the people there. And who gets the credit for all of these changes? President Ronald Reagan. The armaments' build-up that he led forced the Soviets to keep up. But the Soviets couldn't, and Gorbachev had to make the changes he did in order to save the economy.

"Go ol' Ronnie!" is what I wrote in my journal that evening.

We then re-entered West Berlin through the East Berlin border crossing at Friedrichstrasse. "Guards still almost pleasant, no weapons in sight. Amazing feeling – freedom." Gerhard drove his car through Potsdammer Platz and met us in West Berlin. I wrote: "We've come a long way, baby!"

But all wasn't good news on the international scene. The news media in Berlin kept people informed during these most joyous days about Romania: 3,000-4,000 dead in the uprising to overthrow Nicolae Ceausescu. We saw hand-lettered posters urging Berliners not to forget the Romanian people. One banner even said not to celebrate too much when the Romanians are suffering so.

And the U.S. invasion of Panama, with more than 300 dead, was also headlined in the Berlin papers. "Will it ever stop?" was the question I asked myself concluding my journal entry of

December 20.

We also visited a very interesting site. *Treibwerk* is the name given to what became the "graffiti center" of Berlin. It was located in East Berlin and had become the center for protests in 1989: Posters and photographs supporting the *Die Wende* were now on display. On December 21 we all went there just to see what it was like. My journal entry: "Four months ago this all would not have been allowed. Unbelievable!"

The Palace of the Republic was the Democratic Republic's parliament building; it was very modern, having been constructed in the mid-1970s. We just had to go there. My journal entry from that evening included: "Nice building, stale social art called 'The Communist Dreams.' Even made Jürgen laugh."

(Not to forget: Jürgen, in the mid-1980s, was the most supportive of my friends of the socialist regime. He was definitely experiencing his own *Wende*.)

The entire Palace of the Republic was razed in 2007, eventually to be replaced with an art and cultural center.

That evening of December 21 we were all invited to Barbara's apartment, where she'd been since September, for dinner. It was typical of what a young person could afford then: an entryway, one large room, small kitchen, and a bedroom; she had no furniture since she'd just painted the place. She and Jürgen prepared the dinner: roast goose, red cabbage, potatoes, fruit salad and, of course, wine, a Hungarian wine. The room was lit with eight candles of various sizes; the music of Beethoven played on the record player. We ate at a round, outdoor table that she had brought in. From my journal entry describing the evening: "Quiet enjoyment of wonderful friendship. And now they're free. Lots of laughs."

Ivan, Gerhard and I left around 9:45 but turned the wrong way. As we drove back past her apartment, Barbara and Jürgen were dancing in the street. I wrote, "Wow. What a different feeling, to know that they can all leave and travel and come to the West at will. No more goodbyes at the border. Thank you, God."

December 22 arrived along with a cold rain and a temperature of 45 F, typical for Berlin in December. We went to the celebration at the Brandenburg Gate; it was to be opened to pedestrian traffic by 5:00 that afternoon; speeches by the mayors of both Berlins, and Chancellor Helmut Kohl of West Germany were on the agenda.

I wanted to climb up on top of the Wall, but there was literally no room; hundreds, perhaps thousands, were already up there. An announcement came over the loud speakers, prefaced by the German phrase: *Liebe Mauerblümchen!* ("Dear little flowers of the Wall.") All were encouraged to be very careful, because with so many on top of the Wall, it could be very dangerous. Soon people were asked to get down; it was just too crowded. I'll never forget how East Berlin border guards and West Berlin police worked together to help people, even getting a ladder. A ladder on the east side of the Berlin Wall to help people get down: simply unbelievable!

At about 4:30 the crowd was permitted to walk through an opening in the Wall, through the Brandenburg Gate and into East Berlin. A beautiful scene: people singing, cheering, hugging; television floodlights, flags, and posters proclaiming the unity of Berlin and of the two Germanys; and, of course, champagne.

The East German border personnel also seemed to be enjoying the whole scene. We had our picture taken with them – something that a couple of months before would have never have been permitted. They were happy to do it. One of them even said to me: *Wenn die Engel reisen, weint der Himmel.* In English: "When angels travel, heaven cries." (It's a wish for good luck and a safe journey when one leaves on a trip and it's raining.) Another, who told me he had been an East German officer since the 1960s, said: *Wir sind ein Volk.* – "We are one people."

Another poster: *Habe Staat, suche Volk* - "I've got a country, looking for a people."

More announcements from a loudspeaker truck: lost children, lost purses, lost grandmothers, etc.

A very interesting character dressed as a fairy with wings, a dress and large earrings rode a unicycle that put him well above the crowd.

A row of 15-20 portable toilets, just in case.

Celebrators striking at the east side of the Wall with broken street barriers that used to keep people away from the Wall; they were not as efficient as a hammer and chisel, though.

And the Berliners weren't just focused on themselves: A great cheer went up from the crowd when it was announced that Ceausescu in Romania had been overthrown.

The first time I saw the Brandenburg Gate was in 1966. During several trips to Berlin over the next 23 years, I was never able to get near it, let alone stand under it. But now I was able to get close, to actually stand between two of its huge columns.

Tears came to my eyes.

But these were tears of joy, not the same tears that we had previously experienced at the "Palace of Tears."

Gerhard took Ivan and me to the train station, we said our good-byes, and were soon on our way to Frankfurt for our flight back to the USA. But this time our parting was not sad; we knew we would be seeing each other in the not too distant future, possibly in California.

We flew home on December 24. Back in Berlin, on Christmas day, Leonard Bernstein would lead the Berlin Philharmonic in Beethoven's Ninth Symphony, *An die Freude* - "Ode to Joy." But he would change the title for this performance: It was now *An die Freiheit* - "Ode to Freedom."

We had spent an incredible and unforgettable five days in a soon to be reunited Berlin. I remember so clearly passing through Customs at the Dallas airport. "Where y'all been?" asked the customs' officer. "Berlin," was the answer. "Wow – good trip?" "Yes, it was great. Would you like a piece of the Wall?" "Why, sure!"

He got a piece; I hope he still has it.

Before boarding our flight to Los Angeles, I took a walk around the airport, re-entering, one could say. We were almost home. A professional football game was on the bar TV: Oakland Raiders 27, New York Giants 17. Life continued in the good old US of A. I was no longer in Berlin, but so thankful to have just experienced it.

The Wall's Fall

Brandenburg Gate in December, 1989.

Celebrating on the Wall at Brandenburg Gate, December 22, 1989.

"Daddy, can I have a piece of the Wall, too?"

Author David Strack chipping at the Wall, December 1989.

Posters announcing the big festival to celebrate *Ost und West* coming together.

East and West Berlin border police helping celebrants off the Wall.

Many dressed up to celebrate, including this "Wall Fairy" riding a unicycle.

December 22, 1989, East German border guard helped people get off the Wall.

Graffiti-covered, west side of the Wall…

…and untouched, east-side of the Wall.

CHAPTER THIRTEEN

1990

A wonderful family Christmas came and went. Shortly thereafter, I received a New Year's greeting from Jutta. It wasn't a long and detailed letter about all the changes her country was experiencing, just a very sincere wish for a successful and healthy 1990. Here's what she wrote in her own hand, with the English translations:

Ein erfülltes und gesundes Jahr 1990

A fulfilled and healthy 1990

*Frieden, Hoffnung Abrüstung– und für uns hier
endlich eine deutsche Zukunft*

Peace, hope, disarmament– and for us here
finally a German future

The momentous event that took place in Berlin on November 9, 1989 led to tremendous euphoria throughout East Germany. In the following weeks, thousands drove their "Trabis" into West Germany, France, Holland and other Western European countries; others took trains, planes and busses, exercising their newly granted travel rights. They were finally experiencing the freedom they had desired for so long, and for which they had protested. Those who could afford it, booked flights to America and other overseas destinations. And so many looked forward to the further changes that a democratic, non-socialist economic and political system would bring, not the least of which were freedom of speech, assembly, and the press.

* * *

The first "post Fall" letter I received was from Jürgen, dated February 15, 1990. But things aren't quite as he had expected:

> Right now I'm worried about my job. The first unemployed are beginning to appear here now, and one doesn't know who's going to be next. Our editorial office here in Leipzig is being done away with, and I've not been offered a new position.
>
> Times are very unsettled here now, and we're also worried about our money. And I don't feel any better when I hear Federal Chancellor Kohl speak: I'm not sure a quick re-unification is the best course to take right now. I'll keep you informed about all of this in due time.

* * *

Jutta, however, consistently had a much more positive outlook. (Remember, it was she who had received permission to travel to West Germany as early as 1988.) This was in spite of the fact that she and Andreas were getting divorced or, as she put it, experiencing "Andreas' exodus from our family."

1990 was going to be a year of "great political events, disarmament, and steps toward freedom all around the world. . ."

She also wrote something that I found very interesting and quite personal. This dealt with changing her son's name:

> By the way: my baby's name is no longer Sebastian, but Jakob. That name "fits" better in the Jewish-Hebrew line. I just love those names of the Old Testament. And I admire the deep wisdom of the legends and stories found there.

Jutta had already received invitations to visit friends in many places, including Vancouver, Canada. But her children were too young, and she didn't have the funds to allow her to "cross the ocean and explore America." She was very satisfied with traveling to other countries in Europe, "which has suddenly grown so excitingly large for us." A week in Paris was on her itinerary:

> I am excited like a little child before Christmas: reading books on Paris, studying road maps of France, working on my poor French, telling Judith about the famous curiosities of Paris. It's a friend who's invited us there – and he's providing us with a car as a present for our freedom! Isn't that wonderful? Keep your fingers crossed that *Paris* comes true!

Jutta did get to Paris. And in 1998 she and her two sons traveled to California.

The Wall was truly down.

* * *

At the end of March, I received Jürgen's letter written on the 25th. It is three pages long and contains quite detailed reactions to what had been happening in East Germany since November.

He wrote that events were just overwhelming– and that he didn't know where to start.

> I'll start with myself. At the present time I've got just so much to do again because the changes in society are being reflected in our personal lives. Many transformations are raining down at work, the best example of which is that the editorial office in which I work here in Leipzig will not exist as it has previously.

> Through the free market reforms that have been instituted, so much literature from the Federal Republic is coming into our country that we won't be able to withstand the pressure, and we are going to have to completely transform ourselves. The catalogs and all the stamp-collecting literature that we've been publishing here are being entirely imported from the Federal Republic, and we just can't keep up both in quality and quantity.

He was going to have to work now in the marketing department, representing his company and three others. And it wasn't going to be easy. After three years of a "desk job," he would be going on the road, needing to get a car and a driver's license, in addition to taking computer courses. Having a car would enable him to have direct contact with the people who read their books, but necessitate that he drive all over Germany, "visiting book stores and offering books."

"Welcome to capitalism" was what I thought, but I did not communicate that back to him.

However, things would be very different, and he seemed to be looking forward to that:

> This existential fear is really something new for us here. The social market economy will certainly lead to a lot of unemployment, but that's the way we wanted it! The laggardness of the last years is now taking to a certain extent its revenge. This "new life" also wants to be organized!!

The first free elections in East Germany had been held a week earlier. He thought I'd like to learn what he thought of that. It wasn't what I was expecting:

> Disappointment is spreading. I simply couldn't comprehend that the "Alliance for Germany" [A coalition of opposition parties] won. Unfortunately those who were responsible for the democracy movement of 1989 got the fewest votes. With support from the West, those who made the most promises are now forming the new government. The victor was money. People voted with their stomachs, not with their heads.
>
> The 40% who voted for the conservative Christian Democratic Union thought that with a CDU victory the German Mark would be introduced here on the next day. But far from it. Helmut Kohl, the Federal Chancellor, has already pulled back on some of his promises. A common currency is not coming until perhaps late next summer. And a unified Germany will also take a while, perhaps 3 or 5 or 7 years. But Kohl's got his victory. Unfortunately!

He went on to explain that, in his opinion, the CDU victory

could be attributed to workers, farmers, and those from small villages, out-voting those in the big cities who supported the more liberal parties: the Socialist Party of Germany (SPD) and the Party of Democratic Socialism (PDS). (I know it's confusing.)

"But we just can't sit around and complain, we've got to accept this result and make the best out of it. My suggestion for the German national anthem now is: *D-Mark, D-Mark über Alles!*"

That's a rather clever change in the actual title of the German National Anthem: *Deutschland, Deutschland über Alles.*

In January, Jürgen "played tour guide" for Astryd Royhus, the German teacher friend from Norway, who had brought a group of her students to Berlin. They met in West Berlin, and he was able to show them around East Berlin. He even got disco tickets for the students so he and Astryd and a colleague could "spend a quiet evening together." Thanks to *Die Wende* he would be visiting her that summer in Norway. And he concluded this letter with: "But wait, my friend, I'll be coming to the USA! Hang on when the Saxons come!" (Saxony is the Federal State where Leipzig is located.)

In 1991 Jürgen visited us in California. And to think that less than three years before we all wondered if the Wall "would ever come down."

Wende, we thank you.

Jürgen wrote on July 27 that he had just come back from a business trip to Berlin when he received my letter that took seventeen days to arrive. I had included prints of photos taken during our time together the previous December. He, too, would never forget the experience we'd all had: "Thank you so much for the photos. Those are true historical documents. The pictures at the Wall will be in a place of honor."

Earlier, you may recall, Jürgen was quite critical of how things were going in early 1990. But now, currency reform, an important step toward unification - which would take place in three months - was clearly on its way:

> You can't imagine how fast things are moving here. When this letter gets to you we'll already have a new currency, which is for us progress into the future, even though we're afraid of what that could all bring. But it's certainly an important step towards a united Europe, and this goal really makes one feel good.

However, there were more important things on our minds that summer. Jürgen wrote: "But today I don't want to write so much about political things, but more about your trip to Berlin this summer."

I was planning another trip to Germany with my students and had informed him of the dates. A very major musical event was to be held on July 21, 1990, in Berlin: Pink Floyd's *The Wall* concert, in outdoor format, was to be performed on Potsdammer Platz, literally next to the Brandenburg Gate and also where the Wall used to be. Attending it was a "must" for my students and me.

Jürgen was starting his summer vacation – a canoeing trip in northern Germany – on that date. We really wanted to get together, especially if it could be at the concert. Canoe trips, however, can be complicated:

> We're leaving Leipzig on July 21 and won't be in Berlin until the evening. I'm so sorry! That means we'll only be in Berlin for the concert because we've got to get our canoes and tents that evening. That means we can't stay in Berlin. The only possibility would be that we meet up at the concert but, to be honest, I don't think that can happen because there will be just so many people there – it seems like everyone from East and West Germany wants to be there.

I didn't see Jürgen at the concert. Too many people: The official attendance was over 200,000. The entire evening consisted of live music played by Roger Waters' group Pink Floyd. The story of their album *The Wall* was projected on a gigantic Styrofoam wall, which represented the actual Wall. It was 100 feet high, one hundred yards long, and collapsed at the end of the evening to the chant of "tear down the wall."

It was an evening we'll never forget.

Three major changes were about to happen in Jürgen's life: He'd applied for a job at another publishing house, but the contract hadn't been signed yet. And he was hoping to get a new apartment and also his own car.

But things weren't going to be easy:

I hope to be getting my own apartment very shortly. There's an empty place here on my street, which I'm interested in. But you have no idea how hard it is here. It can only be done through underhanded tricks. And now I'm going to be doing something that I don't like doing and that I haven't done for a year – own a flat. I guess that's the way it goes. And then I'm in the middle of my driving tests. I had no clue earlier that I was going to need a car. I've got to buy one. I don't know what kind it will be because I'm completely clueless when it comes to mechanical things. But in time it will all work out.

Jürgen was just beginning to experience the changes that many ex-East German citizens would: a non-socialist, free-market economy. It wouldn't be easy for him, but, as we shall see, eventually he did quite well.

His vacation in Mecklenburg was not like in previous years:

It was so peaceful this year for the majority of GDR citizens are now making their way to Spain, Italy, West Germany, Paris, Rome, or the Costa Brava. It's just a wave of travel that has been started and who can blame them, for until now people have only been able to get to know Eastern Europe. It's a beautiful thing and I'm happy that I'm still so young and have life in front of me.

A capitalist economic system requires that people work hard. This is not to imply that Jürgen did not work hard before *Die Wende*. For him, however, the fourteen-hour workday had arrived. "Sometimes I've really had enough of it, but then I just think things are so much better than they were. I'm just overwhelmed now, though."

He used to ride his bicycle to work. Now he has to worry about passing his driver's test and the eventual upkeep of a car. And gas prices in Germany were twice those in the USA.

> I've been driving on Leipzig's streets now for a couple of weeks, making things not really too safe. But it's also great fun, and I'm not having any problems. The big problem now is money. Our salaries were so nicely cut in half in July, and money is slowly becoming quite short, what for driving school, the car, and furnishing my new flat. It's just 24-hour stress: Work, driving school, renovating the apartment, buying furniture, painting, hiring a plumber and on and on.

He did, however, say that some things were considerably cheaper than under the old system. Adequate supplies of carpeting and furniture, for example, were now readily available as they hadn't been in GDR times. This led to the project of renovating his apartment, something he couldn't have done just two years earlier.

He also seemed to like working for the publishing firm that produced automobile books, mainly because he could arrange his time himself. Working at a desk had been brought to a minimum. He was now on the road all day visiting and advising clients. However, since there were no more subsidies, books were four to six times more expensive. But the higher prices hadn't hurt sales volume, for "earlier in GDR times there was nothing like this available here in the book industry."

I wrote earlier that we would see Jürgen eventually doing

quite well; it would take over twenty years.

By 1990, things had improved somewhat. The free market was providing what he needed to renovate his apartment: paint in the colors he wanted, carpeting, nice furniture. And acquiring these items before had meant "months of running around, getting in line at night so one could get a place in the line for the next day. Now shopping is actually at least fun!"

In early October 1990, I wrote to Jürgen and asked him if people were "more content, happier." I wanted to know what the reunification of Germany had brought to the people of the former German Democratic Republic.

His reply was very open and honest. Here are his comments in their entirety:

I'm neither happier than before, nor more content.

On the contrary, I'm very embittered by what's happened in this country. Please understand that I'm only speaking for myself, and this is not a statement that fits all and you shouldn't generalize.

On October 3, 1990 we had the great Day of Unification, a day that brought many celebrations of happiness, even tears of joy. I had no reason to celebrate this day. Why? Because now I'm a "real" German? The end of the GDR was for everybody here a break in his or her life, and no one can forget the last forty years.

People are always talking of "coming to terms with the past." But what is there to come to terms with? "Coming to terms with" can be called change. How does one want to change the past? These 40 years will always be a part of our biography. And that will always distinguish us from those other Germans who happened to be born further to the west.

Believe me, the GDR was not the most horrible thing on the planet. Now at this time people seem to think that this Democratic Republic was the root of utmost evil. Suddenly there's supposed to be nothing here, and also there wasn't any good here. And that really gets me.

Everything, really everything, is supposed to be taken over by the West. That begins with our laws; the constitution has been done away with, fiscal and tax law has been taken over; education is not what it used to be. Schools are being inundated with books from the West. And a solid education for everyone was a badge of honor for us. Gone! Employment is being reduced everywhere. The results: 2.4 million unemployed in the former GDR. In six months. It remains to be seen what the end of the year will bring. Ask the 2.4 million without work if they're more content or happier.

No, dear David, 1989 did not promise us all of this. Many people say here, that's not what we wanted then.

And the population just voted in March. And then the D-Mark.

And Chancellor Kohl. Believe me, these weren't the people who were saying, "We are the people" in 1989. Because then it was about a renewing of the GDR. With open borders, with a market economy.

Those who yelled out "Germany united Fatherland" appeared later, when the old system had already been done away with. I call it *Die Wende nach der Wende*. [The change after the change].

But don't think now that I'm completely unhappy. NO – I'm only unhappy with what's developed!

A difficult struggle has begun. Like with my job: A colleague of mine from those times is now a competitor, whom I've got to outbid in order to keep my job. But that's business. I just don't like it. I'm certainly earning basically more money than before. But that all goes for necessities. There's nothing left over for savings. Priority is now my car payments.

But don't worry – I'm not going to starve.

Then the word "freedom" occurs to me. Yes, now I can travel the whole world. This freedom I have. Better: I could have! Yes – I could travel, but the financial means are missing. We're paying now the same that one paid in the old Federal Republic, the same prices for services; only our wages haven't increased in the same proportion. I've got to watch my money every day. Before I didn't have to do that.

And you ask if I'm happier or more content!!??

But there's still the one and only hope that life here will soon normalize. The financial experts tell us of a "bottoming out" (how romantic!) in 5 to 7 years. And from where are we to get our optimism?

Uphill progress - climbing – is being made here only in the mountains.

Jürgen normally typed his entire letter. But this time the concluding statement was in his own handwriting. I think he did it for emphasis:

You see, everything has its advantages and disadvantages. I hope I haven't made too much of a pessimistic impression. In 7 years all will be forgotten!!! So long!

I'm not sure all was forgotten by 1997, but life seemed to be better for most people still living in "Old East Germany." In

1992, my wife and I visited Jürgen in his re-furbished apartment in Leipzig; he was a most gracious host, and seemed quite content with how his life was going.

But more on that later.

* * *

I received a Christmas card and New Year's greeting from Gerhard in December. What I didn't expect to be included were two pictures: One he entitled: "Biking on the Death Strip." Yes – people riding their bikes in the area along the Wall that I earlier referred to as "no man's land." The second was of a "unification celebration" in a small village in eastern Germany. (I regret I don't have the pictures now.) Gerhard seemed to be more pleased with Unification than Jürgen was. At least at the end of 1990.

CHAPTER FOURTEEN

1991

The first letter I received in 1991 was from Jutta. Contrary to Jürgen's rather critical descriptions of what was happening, she was extremely enthusiastic about the changes taking place in her life. Her younger son, Jakob, was now in pre-school; she was continuing her study of Spanish, Swedish and French; she wanted to be able to "cope with the new era which holds its doors wide open for the world, for an entire Europe." She was just as enthusiastic about freedom and the new opportunities it presented, as she was when she had first traveled to Frankfurt two years earlier.

Her summer travel plans to Denmark had already been made; a trip to the Mediterranean in the fall was also planned. "It's wonderful! It's great to travel around and to get to know beautiful Europe!"

Before asking me to keep in touch and to forgive her eventual breaks in our correspondence, she concludes her letter with this:

I'm well, I'm free and easy, enjoying all my children, freedom, my dreams and plans, and the plentitude of what is possible for us "Easterners" makes me happy and hopeful.

How I smiled when I read those words.

* * *

Jürgen also wrote in March, just two days after Jutta did. He apologized for not having written in a while, explaining how busy he was at work: He hadn't read a book for months, would come home "totally beat," open up a beer and watch television. He seemed to always be busy fixing up his new apartment: drilling holes, hanging curtains, putting books into shelves, and unpacking. Plans included an open-house party; but it just wasn't going to happen soon. His criticism of the changes brought by *Die Wende* continued:

But the desire to have a party just isn't here for me yet. People are all so frustrated; all are worried because after one and a half years of democracy and justice, things just aren't as we had imagined they would be. Nobody knows how much rent they'll have to pay, everything's just up in the air and that's making people rather *kaputt*.

And in addition, 100,000 workers have come to Saxony – over two-thirds of them have only part-time jobs. And while not working full-time, they still get money from the state.

People are very disappointed in the new society. Perhaps you've read: We're having Monday demonstrations again here in Leipzig, like before *Die Wende*. And on Monday there were just as many people as then – 75,000. And I think there will be even more next Monday. This time the federal government won't be so pleased with these demonstrators, because the protest is not against a communist regime, but against this government, which was elected a year ago by the people because they were promised heaven on earth. People bought into it – and now we all have practically nothing. Do you remember my letter of a year ago? I know how I complained about how naïve people were; that they chose the D-Mark and voted with their stomachs. And now we're seeing the results of this political movement: massive unemployment, angst about one's existence, social disadvantage for us former East Germans.

And those in the West say all we've got to do is roll up our sleeves and go for it. That's an insult; we're working here like crazy and have got to listen to such advice???

Everybody is frustrated.

He concluded this letter with hearty greetings and best wishes for my health and that of my friend from our original "Berlin group," Ivan – who was very ill at the time. "I hope he's better now – my thoughts are with him."

Ivan recovered. And so did Germany.

* * *

I received a letter from Jutta in October. I was, and still am amazed, at her positive attitude toward the events in Germany that were obviously causing problems for many of her fellow citizens. She had just returned from a relaxing vacation on the Spanish island of Ibiza in the Mediterranean, where "one could swim and walk around without gloves," for temperatures were then approaching freezing in Germany. Her joy of freedom seemed boundless:

> For me the greatest joy was to speak Spanish. You know I've always enjoyed learning foreign languages, and it was caused by my desire to be free and to maybe talk freely then to foreign people. So you can probably imagine what impetus our newly won freedom means for my language studies!
>
> I'm taking refresher courses in French, too, and I've re-started Swedish. We've also had guests from Canada, the U.S., Sweden, and Italy and we had such a nice time together. These prospects are marvelous! Of course there's so much still to explore for us Easterners! I think Europe is large enough for the very beginners!

She wrote that she was also starting her doctoral studies on the works of the Australian playwright Jack Hibberd; she hoped to receive scholarship support either from the University of Leipzig or from Australia itself.

In December Jutta reported she had received a three-year scholarship to pursue her degree. She could now work on her thesis "without financial sorrows."

Here is her concluding paragraph from this letter, written on December 18, 1991:

> We finish this year, conscious of how lucky we are to be free to travel, free to shape our own lives, to send our children to schools not tied to ideological oppression.
>
> We traveled to Denmark and to Spain– isn't it wonderful after

all those dark and hopeless years…?

People are largely moaning about their salaries still being at lower levels than the Western ones; they have quickly forgotten the misery they've come from. . . That's people! For me, the new existential dimensions of being are still as amazing and marvelous as they were on the very first day. This awareness is not common, but I keep thinking of those Eastern Europeans who won't see increasing life levels, travels, and convertible money during the next decade…

Who were these "Eastern Europeans" who, in Jutta's opinion, were not yet experiencing the freedoms she was? I assumed she meant primarily the Russians, who, while experiencing positive change, were still living under Soviet rule when she wrote this letter.

So – two years had passed since *Die Wende*. I found it very interesting that Jürgen and Jutta were of such diverse views and opinions: Jürgen was critical of virtually everything; Jutta loved her new-found freedom so much that she was already making plans to study in Australia.

In a few years, as we shall see, even Jürgen's life would improve because of what had happened in 1989.

David F. Strack

CHAPTER FIFTEEN

1992

In July Bonnie and I were again in Leipzig. I had written to Jürgen, telling him that we would be making the trip and wanted very much to see him. We had no problem staying in a hotel and were looking forward to possibly having dinner with him and seeing some sites of the city. He would have no part of that:

> I was really happy to get your postcard, particularly to read that you want to come to Leipzig again. You just can't believe how glad I was to hear from you.
>
> About lodging: In any case you'll be my guests. I have an apartment that's big enough. I won't allow you to refuse!!! It would be just crazy to spend money on a room. As far as I'm concerned you can have the whole place. It's got three rooms. *Not a problem at all!*

This was the apartment he had moved into a year before and was so busy renovating, installing new carpeting, painting, repairing, etc. We had an absolutely perfect stay and we were so very grateful. Our time in Leipzig included visiting some key sites of the city: St. Thomas church, where J.S. Bach was minister of music; the Nicholas Church, where the demonstrations which set

Die Wende in motion began; Auerbachs Restaurant, the first place in Goethe's *Faust* to which Mephistopheles (the devil) takes Faust on their travels, attempting to win over his soul.

Leipzig is a beautiful city, so rich in history and culture. And having not been in Leipzig for nearly ten years made our stay with Jürgen even nicer.

His apartment was not big: one bedroom, a living room, and kitchen. It was very well appointed: nice furniture and bookshelves, stereo, television, beautiful ceramic coal-burning heater, comfortable and clean. But no toilet. Yes, no toilet. It was in a small enclosure on the landing between the third and fourth floors, his apartment being on the fourth. Shower? No shower, but a bathtub that pulled down out of a wall in the kitchen. Yes, that's where we bathed, in the kitchen bathtub. (Naturally after Jürgen had prepared, and we had eaten, breakfast!)

Our stay was so very much appreciated, and we'll never forget our time with him. I don't remember his being so critical of his situation, as he had been in his previous letters. Maybe we just avoided the topic.

* * *

Jutta's desire to travel and to take advantage of her freedom continued to be the highest priority for her. She informed me in June that she had received her scholarship to study in Melbourne,

Australia. She wrote, as always in English, about how excited she was:

> You can surely imagine my stirred emotions during these days—all I've been striving for, freedom of such unknown perspective, has become true. I am as moved as ever by these new horizons, and I belong to the ever decreasing number of those Easterners who'd never change freedom against what was before; even if it would offer me only bread and water each day.

That statement – "the ever decreasing number of those Easterners who'd never change freedom against what was before" - said to me that she understood the problems with which many East Germans were dealing: inflation, high unemployment, greatly increased rents, etc. But to her, freedom was completely worth it. She was going to raise her children in a free society, get her education, and travel the world.

As we shall learn later, she succeeded.

* * *

Jürgen, on the other hand, was still very upset with what was happening in the former Democratic Republic. On December 12 he began his letter as follows:

> As you've read in the newspaper, life here in the new federal states is pretty hard. Even I have lost my job. My company gave me notice on January 1, but I've applied for a new position and everything isn't complete yet, because some

decisions still have to be made by the company. Perhaps I'll become self-employed or I'll try something completely different.

Here are some statistics he included:

-7,000 teachers have been let go.

-13,000 more teachers will lose their jobs in 1993.

-His rent is 270 Marks per month. It had been 40.

-Prices for energy – coal and gas – increase monthly.

As Gerhard, Barbara and Jutta also did, he appreciated his freedom now to travel, but: "What good is it that I can now possibly travel to the USA, but I don't have any money to do it?"

(Jürgen eventually got the money together to travel, arriving in California in the summer of 1993. But more on that later.)

Here's a rather long German word: *Staatssicherheitsdienst*. It translates into English as "State Security Service." It was the East German secret police, simply known as the *Stasi*. The Stasi's purpose was to ensure "state security." And to achieve that it had an extensive spy network that secretly observed GDR citizens, and participated in other activities designed to protect the State. I was never aware of any Stasi activities regarding my friends or me. But that doesn't mean there weren't any.

Something one can do now is get access to one's "Stasi files." It's a rather involved process, but it can be done. I've thought about it, but have never had the opportunity. I would only do it out of curiosity, not because I believe there is anything "dangerous" in the file. (I doubt very much there even is a file on me.)

I later learned that it could take up to three years to get access to one's file. It's very possible that all of my East German friends, however, do have Stasi files. We never discussed this when we were together. Only Jürgen mentioned the possibility of seeing his file. I found his comment very interesting:

People are also concerned about the situation with the Stasi files. That's for sure. One now has the possibility to make a request to look at one's file, then there's a long waiting period, and then one can read what was put in there over the years. I don't want to see my file. What good is it for me to know which colleague, which family member, which friend worked for the Stasi? And that just brings more frustration. And I don't want to live with that knowledge – there's much more that is really more important to me.

David F. Strack

CHAPTER SIXTEEN

1993

In February of 1993, Jürgen wrote what led me to believe that he was becoming, for lack of a better term, a capitalist:

> Here is the most important news: I struck out on my own in December, started my own small firm, which is made up of one person – me. And you can imagine what a tremendous amount of work that has been. I've also stayed on with Bartelsmann [a publishing firm] and am a contractor with them. If this will be something for the future, only the stars know.

> There's such a huge German bureaucracy I have to deal with, and that means there is a tremendous amount of things to go through with the public authorities, and especially "enjoyable" was working with the finance ministry where every fart has to be proved with documentation. Terrible!

Ah – the thoroughness of German bureaucracy!

And he was also very busy with the continued renovation of his apartment: Finally a bathroom so the tub did not have to be pulled down, out the kitchen wall; a toilet not in a little room between floors; a new heating system where "I only have to set the temperature and the place gets quite cozy and doesn't get so dirty." Even the façade of the building was being renovated. "Everything is being cleaned. It will look really nice."

In the early 1990s my correspondence and contact with Gerhard, Jürgen, Barbara, and Jutta just about ceased. They were adjusting to new jobs and life styles; travel had become very important. I even led my last student trip to Germany in 1995, but did not make contact with them. I guess we all got so "busy with life" that letter-writing just didn't get done. I truly believed they were fine, healthy and enjoying their freedom.

Letter writing had taken a back seat, so to speak, to travel. Three of them – Gerhard, Jürgen, and Jutta - all came to California.

Gerhard was the first to visit. "David, I want to see lots of California – show me," was his basic request. I was very happy to show him more than just Southern California. We visited the mountains near our hometown, the deserts near Palm Springs, and the Pacific Ocean at La Jolla, where our friend Ivan, who was recovering from a very serious illness, lived. This naturally included San Diego. And that's not far from Tijuana, Mexico. *"Vamos a Mexico!!"*

We spent half a day there shopping, walking around, and doing more shopping.

And then we were off to the Grand Canyon. The drive across the high desert north of Flagstaff, Arizona, was incredible. "Wow– we don't have this in Germany!" was one of Gerhard's comments as he saw this beautiful landscape; and then we arrived at the Canyon on a perfectly clear spring day: tears came to Gerhard's eyes when we first stood on the rim. He later told me - when we were together in Berlin during the 25th anniversary celebration of the fall of the Wall – that at that moment on the rim of the Grand Canyon – he just couldn't control his emotions:

> It suddenly just hit me how much had been taken away from me, how much I hadn't been allowed to experience, because I'd lived in East Germany for so many years.

Our trip continued as we drove back to California and then south along the Colorado River from Lake Havasu. I remember he took photographs of the big-rig trucks on the interstate. "Amazing – our trucks in Germany are not so huge!"

It was truly a memorable experience for both Gerhard and me. Our contacts and letter writing didn't stop – even though there was a rather long pause in the exchange of physical letters. Our correspondence eventually picked up again with email.

(His comments on how his life is going today are very interesting. I'll summarize those later in this narrative.)

* * *

Jürgen was the next former East German to visit us in California. Taking advantage of his newfound freedom to travel, he spent a week in California in the spring of 1993.

He summarized this trip in a recent email: He remembers being in the High Desert near us, where he experienced temperatures that he didn't think existed: 104 Fahrenheit; Big Bear Lake – at an elevation of 7,000 feet – where there was still snow on the ground; San Diego and La Jolla, where we visited my friend Ivan; riding the roller-coaster at Mission Beach near San Diego; purchasing a pullover sweater at Quicksilver. He also enjoyed a barbecue with our friends, time in our Jacuzzi, and apple pie in near-by Oak Glen. "You see, David, there's still so much about that trip that I remember."

In his letters of the 1980s and early 1990s Jürgen was quite critical of the West, and its role in the arms' race. And he was never a fan of the capitalist economic system. He even, as we have read, had his doubts if what was happening in Germany after the fall of the Wall was for the better.

I believe that the freedom he was now experiencing in being able to travel to America was the beginning of a complete change in his outlook on life. He is now employed by Radio Leipzig and seems quite pleased with his situation in life. More on that later.

After the Wall

City bus going through opened Brandenburg Gate.

Free-flowing traffic going through Checkpoint Charlie.

Taxis passing freely through Brandenburg Gate.

Tourists getting their souvenir pieces of the Wall. (1990)

Climbing on Wall's remains. (1990)

Current view from where Checkpoint Charlie stood. (2008)

David F. Strack

CHAPTER SEVENTEEN

The E-Mail Letters

It's amazing how fast time passes. Nearly two decades passed with hardly any correspondence that consisted of letters sent through the postal services. While we exchanged Christmas and New Year's greetings, we all seemed to get so busy that regular letter writing stopped. I was even wondering if one of my friends, Gerhard, was still alive; a letter to him was returned as "undeliverable."

Enter computers and email.

I had not heard from Gerhard for nearly twenty years. But our mutual friend Linda – one of the original contact persons in Berlin in 1974 – did have his email address and was able to get it to me.

In October of 2012, I received this email that made me so very happy because Gerhard and I were again in contact:

My heart skipped a beat when I saw the email from you. I got a couple of emails from Linda, and Stefan [Linda's husband] figured out that I as a dummy used the wrong address. But then a week went by without hearing from her and also nothing from you and I thought: "That's probably it." She told David something and now the two of them are mad at me. But now I'm really relieved.

Without my even asking something like "How are you doing, old boy?" Gerhard caught me up on his life:

So – how am I doing? Measured against the rest of the world I live in pure luxury. But in Germany I'm definitely in the lower social class. And the reason for this has to do with the political situation and me. At age 55 [1998] I'd had it with the treadmill of where I was working and with the looming vulture of capitalism. My senior boss was a fair man, but his son was a moral pig who literally walked over bodies. He bought out an East Berlin firm for one Euro and closed the one in West Berlin. I didn't go, got rid of my apartment, took my savings and traveled around Europe.

When I turned 60 my money was gone and I immediately retired.

Since I had worked for the longest time in the GDR and retired too soon I couldn't get full retirement benefits. But that didn't matter– it was enough for a modest life without extras. No car, also no women and now I live a "second hand" life. I'm happy with Internet connection and television. Otherwise I've got loose contacts and my hobby is buying computer parts at the flea market cheaply and then rebuilding them into functioning PCs. Sometimes people who have problems with their computers help me by paying me to fix them. But there's really no profit in this because they are also so poor.

I don't know if this interests you, but that's how it is with me now. If somebody asks me how I'm doing, and it's someone I know well, my answer is "just fine."

Gerhard then concluded, writing: "I'm not sure how important all of this is and in order to avoid any more negative comments, I'll close for today."

Definitely important, and yes, negative, but I appreciated his honesty.

Gerhard's next email was written three days later, on October 7th. I had told him what I was doing with all the letters from my "old East German friends." I must have written something asking about any experiences they might have had with the Stasi, the East German security police. Gerhard had two:

It was probably in 1988 when the police in civilian clothes appeared at where I worked. When they saw me they said the issue was over because I didn't have any tattoos on my arms. They told me that a woman who had been raped had recognized me in a file as her assailant. But he had tattoos.

His second experience was when he got home one day and noticed that the dictionary he'd received from our friend Linda was not in its normal place. It was in the hall closet.

Here is his account of what he believed happened:

You've got to know that in those times in was forbidden for GDR citizens to have printed materials from the West. It was clear to me that the Stasi had broken into my apartment, having determined beforehand that I wouldn't be home. They took a bunch of letters of my correspondence with the USA. Maybe they even installed listening devices, I don't know. They were looking for reasons to stick me in prison. But they apparently recognized the fact that I was harmless. It was this "forgotten dictionary" that was the only sign that told me someone had been in my apartment, because such a break-in was also forbidden in the GDR.

That's enough of that.

In this email he also briefly wrote again about his being able to travel to West Berlin in August 1989.

> I was even later permitted without complications to travel to West Berlin. I got permission, but they didn't know I had decided to stay there. People who applied for exit visas had to wait a long time and had to endure all kinds of harassment before they were permitted to leave – or not.

Gerhard finished with these two sentences: "In my next email I'd like to set some things straight about the fall of the Wall. It wasn't only joy, but something occurred that I was afraid would happen."

He later wrote and explained his disappointment with Germany and how things developed after reunification.

He retired in 2003 at the age of 60, which meant a reduction in his pension because he'd taken early retirement. Having worked most of his life in the GDR became a "minus factor" for his income; working for so many years in East Germany meant his retirement base amount was not what it would have been had he worked entirely in the Federal Republic.

He also has no car and "I ride a bicycle now and don't get out of Berlin at all." But in spite of all this: "I've still got a sunny disposition, and no real health problems have popped up."

He continued with his opinion of the situation that

developed in Germany as a result of reunification:

It was clear that bringing the GDR up to a level of West Germany would be very expensive. All the other West Berliners and I had to pay an 8% Berlin tax and at the same time a solidarity tax of 7.5% that was used to build up the East. Consequence: 500 Marks less income per month. Because of that, I wasn't all that happy about the fall of the Wall.

I need to remind the reader here that immediately after the Wall fell, Gerhard was extremely happy about what had happened; he took two trips to California in the early 1990s and enjoyed them very much. But a reality he was not comfortable with eventually set in:

Then the topic of East Germans in general: When they finally got West German marks they naturally only bought products produced in West Germany, and things that they at one time had produced themselves were not purchased. The result of this was that they sawed off the tree limb they were all sitting on.

This email concluded with his opinion – not at all positive – of the situation in Germany since 1989:

And then the great uproar took place. Money is everything and businesses brought themselves down. In addition to this, an army of conmen set off to the East. They were auto salesmen, real estate agents and insurance salesmen, to name just a few. The Easterners believed that these folks were coming from the West to give them gifts and to help them. But they were just a bunch of crooks that pursued a kind of gold rush to exploit the Easterners and to cash in on aid payments in an unjustifiable way. The damages reached into the billions. It was for a long time a region of lawlessness; the East police were ignored or lambasted, judges didn't care anymore and no punishments were handed down. Just like the Wild West.

I think he'd gotten something off of his chest, so to speak. This email ended abruptly:

"Many greetings for today from Gerhard."

The second of these "here's what my life is like today" emails was written on March 10, 2012. He attached two articles from the magazine *Der Spiegel* that dealt with "Reunification Criminality," writing that he'd had "no idea how bad things were and how high the level of criminality was."

Two terms need to be defined here: *Wessi* and *Ossi*. *Wessis* are the Germans who live in West Germany; *Ossis* live in East Germany.

Gerhard wrote that I was "probably more interested in what people felt" after the fall of the Wall. That was very true. His opinion of what happened did open my eyes a bit:

The nation was divided in the heads of people into *Wessis* and *Ossis*. *Wessis* weren't very much interested in reunification - except for the families that had been separated. They looked upon the *Ossis* with great suspicion. *Ossis* naturally used their new freedom, as long as their exchanged money lasted, to travel all over the world, but attracted a lot of attention because of their loutish behavior. Others turned against the East, used the price differentials with Poland and the Czech Republic, making lots of money. The street trade in the Czech Republic was notorious, where one could get the cheapest sex;

pedophiles could do their thing without being hindered. And then there were the bazaars: fake brand-named goods and tobacco products were offered at half-price and sold in great quantities.

What Gerhard wrote reminded me of a "fake brand-named goods' experience" Bonnie and I had in Poland in the mid-1990s. We had taken a day trip with Gerhard from Berlin to visit some friends of his. We stopped at an outdoor market/bazaar just to see what was available. It was quite interesting, well attended, and all items seemed to be reasonably priced. And then we saw the table with *Levi's* Jeans. Except they were *Live's* Jeans. Just a minor misspelling, I guess. They actually did look quite authentic; and they weren't that expensive.

We didn't buy any.

Gerhard continued to fill me in on how his life had changed since 1989. (Remember– he was able to get to West Berlin in August of 1989, roughly four months before the big event.) Hardly anybody in Germany believed in the summer of 1989 that the Berlin Wall would ever be eliminated; it just didn't seem possible. He was looking forward to a new life in a country that was actually foreign to him: West Germany. East Germany – the German Democratic Republic – could have lasted forever, as far as he knew. But it didn't.

And his life changed.

For me personally, a world collapsed with the fall of the Wall.

Half of my life I dreamed of living in the West and now I was back again in the middle of the East [the city of Berlin] with few advantages, which were outweighed by disadvantages.

This is then his situation after November 1989: He has a meager pension and no car; he is an *Ossi* living in the West and has to bear the expense of supporting the East; he does not have enough money to travel, as he would like.

But he is free.

And this freedom, which he got in 1989, is still very much appreciated and so important to him:

But along with all that, I'm doing better today than ever. However, I think of how I could be doing if the Wall were still standing. But at least I had a couple of months of bliss like I had known when I had just fallen in love. I could have, as they say, hugged the whole world.

What I particularly noticed in West Berlin: people smiled. It was the feeling of "we're in the same boat" and are going to make the best out of it. Yes – I came with nothing to West Berlin, a suitcase with a few things. That was it. No money, no work, no apartment, but a bag full of hopes, and that after a short time I would be enjoying the new freedom.

Thanks to you and your invitation, I could hop over the Atlantic and my dream was fulfilled. That's why I cried when I saw the Grand Canyon. Everything was just going through my head. A little bit of rage toward the GDR was also there.

I just can't forget that first view of the Grand Canyon and regret nothing. With Google Earth I can go anywhere.

But there just aren't any high points; nothing more is happening in my life. I'm doing fine– not going hungry or freezing and that's something.

When I read those words, it helped me better understand what had happened to the people of Germany after *Die Wende*. Everything did not work out as one might have expected. Gerhard just wasn't as satisfied with the "New Germany" that Jürgen, Jutta, and Barbara were. But after so many years of not having any contact with him, I was happy to learn that he was alive, healthy and making a life for himself, albeit as a pensioner with a very limited income.

In a more recent email – February 2014 – Gerhard also commented on socialism and the Cold War in a very important historical context:

> Now I also understand how inhumane all of socialism was, and in order to keep its grip on Europe an atomic war was part of the calculation. That Europe wouldn't have been inhabitable probably did not interest the higher-ups at all. Luckily nothing happened and both sides kept their wits about them.

History tells us how important the demonstrations in Leipzig of 1989 were: This peaceful revolution – *Die Wende*, the "change of direction" - led directly to the opening of the Berlin Wall and its destruction; the Soviet Union's days were numbered, and the Cold War would be officially over, with its collapse in December, 1991.

Gerhard understands this and appreciates it now.

* * *

My correspondence with Jürgen in Leipzig was also re-established in 2011 through email. It bears remembering that in 1990 he was, like Gerhard, also very critical of the changes that *Die Wende* had brought to the citizens of the former German Democratic Republic: higher taxes, soaring unemployed, rent increases of 700%, energy costs rapidly increasing. He also wrote that in "five to seven years" everything will have "bottomed out and maybe things would be fine."

Things worked out fine for Jürgen. Here are some of his activities in 2011:

- Vacation in Dubai and Oman with friends, camping in tents, riding quads and camels.
- Two weeks in Italy, spending his summer vacation, also with friends, in Tuscany while visiting Florence, Siena, San Gimignano, and Montepulcano.

He was, and still is, working at Radio Leipzig. "It's always fun and I like going to work. Except I don't have to work today: It's Reformation Day, a holiday."

I had written to him that I was translating all of the letters from my East German friends into English. His comment:

It's great that you're translating the letters. But it's a little embarrassing for me. What did I write? Man– that was almost 30 years ago!!! In the meantime we've celebrated 20 years of reunification. I feel very lucky because I'm doing so well! That I can vacation in Italy and Oman, that I have a car, an apartment across from the park– all that would have never been possible in GDR times.

David – I hope you're doing just as well!

In a subsequent email, I attached one of the letters I had translated. His comment: "Oh my God [in English] – we were so 'political!' I couldn't remember all of that– it's been such a long time!"

* * *

I received another email from Gerhard in 2011. To review a bit, his hobby is using and fixing computers, which means he's very Internet-savvy. I had to smile when I read this:

I could hardly believe it that you were expecting snow in Yucaipa. I looked at pictures on the web-cam: horrible weather. Is it often so? When I was there it rained only once, but it was freezing.

It's amazing how we are all connected now; communication can be so instantaneous, taking seconds instead of days or weeks.

David F. Strack

CHAPTER EIGHTEEN

2012- 2013

Gerhard was still not pleased with the post-unification situation in Germany in 2012. In an email he included two articles from *Der Spiegel*, Germany's equivalent of *Time*, and wrote this:

> In these articles you got the horrible facts, which came to us through reunification and particularly with the expansion of the European Union.
>
> Russian and Balkan mafias are a product of freedom of movement, and after 9/11 we also have the problems with Muslims. But as a comedian once said: "We bitch at a very high level." That's probably true. It only feels so bad because these are problems made by politicians themselves. The people certainly didn't want it to be this way.

One has to respect how Gerhard feels about the changes *Die Wende* brought to Germany. But, as we've read, he at least describes his situation as "fine," to use, perhaps, an over-used word.

My other East German friends do not share his opinion on how things developed in Germany after Reunification. They seem to be very pleased with their lives now. I believe there are a couple of reasons for this: They are considerably younger, being in their 50s, while Gerhard is 71; they are not retired, depending, as Gerhard is, on a pension that is barely adequate; he lives in a small apartment, has no car, and just enough income to "get by." And they are all still gainfully employed. Barbara even has her doctorate degree. And they love to travel and have the funds to do so.

One more point is worth mentioning: Barbara, Jürgen and Jutta all live in Leipzig, a major city of "old East Germany." Jutta is self-employed and living precarious circumstances, but through an inheritance she and her husband have been able to purchase an apartment, which has led to "substantial financial relief." She is doing just fine now.

As with many cities of the Democratic Republic, Leipzig benefited from the infusion of funds through higher taxes from the former West Germany. This was very expensive for the *Wessis*, but quite beneficial for the *Ossis*. Being a Berliner has clearly given Gerhard a different opinion of what happened.

* * *

In an email from Jürgen, written on June 21st, he caught me up on how things were going:

> I've still got my job with Radio Leipzig and must go to work every day, and I'm enjoying it very much. We've become the number one station in Leipzig – that means we've got more

listeners than any of the other stations in Leipzig!

It was now clear to me that Jürgen had really settled into life in the new Germany. (Remember – he had been extremely critical of the economic changes that came with *Die Wende*.) I guess Radio Leipzig was making a profit.

Capitalism strikes again.

He continued describing travel plans, an activity that had been so severely restricted in GDR times:

> I've got a wonderful goal: my vacation trip. This year I'm flying with friends again to Portugal. We'll spend two weeks on the Algarve Coast in Porto de Mos. I'm really looking forward to this because we were there three years ago and it was great.

He was also quite a fan of the German National Soccer Team. The European Championships were being played when he wrote this email. This convinced me he had finally become a genuine "Reunited German":

> Everybody in Germany is talking about soccer now. The European Championships are all over the news now. You guys in the USA probably just don't realize what a big deal this is. On Friday the Germans are playing Greece in the quarterfinal. It's almost a political issue!!! Germany will again be European champion – we'll just have to see if we can pull it off. Our guys will have to shut out the Greeks and send them packing. We're about to see some really great games.

(For all you soccer fans: The Germans did send the Greeks

packing: 4-2. However, they didn't make the finals, losing 2-1 to Italy in the semi-final match. The championship went to Spain, 4-0, victors over Italy in the final.)

$* * *$

The only friend from Leipzig who did not write regularly was Barbara; I'd last heard from her in 1992. Jürgen wrote and told me she was very busy and doing well, but I missed hearing from her personally.

However, in September 2012, I received an email from her! It had been over twenty years since she'd written, and I was so very pleased we were communicating again.

She'd been busy, having moved and furnished a new apartment, in addition to vacationing on a lake with her entire family. She had also been to "charming and lively" Lisbon, Portugal. But she had also lost my email address, which Jürgen had given her, and "I'm finally getting over my guilt for not writing. So— the evening belongs to you!"

Yes— there's much to tell you because so much time has passed since we ate that Christmas goose in Berlin in 1989.

I was in France for four years at the university in Nice, where I taught German language and literature.

My daughter was born in France and is now studying music at the university prep school here in Leipzig. We moved back to Leipzig in 1997 because her father lives here.

Barbara's language and literature studies in Leipzig and Berlin led to her receiving her doctorate degree and to a very rewarding and fulfilling professional life:

> For a couple of years I was editor-in-chief at a local cultural magazine, *Leipziger Blättern*, until when, in 2004, I started with Ernst Klett – a firm that publishes school books. It's one of the three largest schoolbook publishing houses here in Leipzig. I started as a copy editor and now I am responsible for school texts for the subject of German in our college prep secondary schools and for professional education. I'm also a group leader for the subject of theater training.
>
> The home office is in Stuttgart, which means one has to fly a lot. That's all very time consuming and stressful, but very satisfying as to what I have to do. My colleagues make work quite enjoyable since they're all so nice, and also because there are no dummies, and they're really interesting people.

Barbara then wrote she wishes she'd had more children, but her husband was not in favor of that. Her only child, a 15 year-old daughter, would love to spend a year in the USA as an exchange student, but had decided not to because she would have had to give up her activities in Leipzig: hockey, violin in the orchestra, pop-band, jazz-band. Her great passion is English, "perhaps to keep her distance from her French-socialized mother." However, the exchange experience in the USA still might take place: "At first I was a little afraid that she would suddenly go, then I found it too bad that she changed her mind and stayed here. But all that still could happen – after she's done with school."

It had been many years since we had corresponded. Barbara's conclusion to this email was, I felt, quite sincere:

> I wish you very hearty greetings. I was so happy to hear from you. And also that you stumbled on our letters and are translating them for your family really impresses me!
>
> When one thinks how fast one can communicate over the Atlantic now it almost makes me angry that I've not been in contact for so long. All the best!

* * *

Jutta's Christmas greeting of 2012 was a beautiful card, accompanied by a two page, single-spaced letter written in German, and not the usual English. She summarized all of what she and her family had done in 2012, which included a great deal of travel that never would have been possible were the Wall still standing.

Her travels and experiences are incredible. Here's what she and her family, who treasured their freedom more than anything, were able to accomplish, 23 years after *Die Wende*:

- Bicycling along the Danube in Germany

-Hiking in the Alps and the mountains of the Czech Republic

-Skiing in the Bavarian forest

-A weekend of bicycling with Linda and her husband Stefan
   near Weimar. (Linda is one of the "original Berlin group" of

1974, when these friendships all started.)

-Vacation on the Mediterranean island of Mallorca

-A week on an island in the Baltic

-Visiting sons Jakob and David in Stuttgart and Heidelberg, which included more bicycling

-October vacation on the island of Usedom in the Baltic

Such extensive travels did not stand in Jutta's way of her academic activities. She had received a scholarship to pursue her English studies in Belfast, Ireland, in April. She also continued with her teaching and translation activities throughout 2012, and this would be a "short course in classic Mongolian and Tibetan handwriting." (She was able to do this because of her studies of Mongolian at the University of Leipzig.) She is also still translating English books into German for AmazonCrossing.

Our email correspondence picked up again in 2014, and she described her travel plans for 2015: She will be in Armenia to participate in a seminar on literary translation; this will be followed by a trip to Southern China, traveling the Yangtze river; she and husband, Michael, will also visit monasteries in Tibet; then it's "back to Katmandu, crossing the Himalayas, passing Mt. Everest."

* * *

My East German friends are truly amazing. They've all,

particularly Jürgen, Jutta and Barbara, adapted to the New Germany that *Die Wende* brought. This wasn't easy, but with personal discipline and education, they lead successful and what appear to be comfortable lives. Only Gerhard seems to be not too happy with how things have developed in Germany.

Jürgen, Jutta, and Barbara are employed at professional levels that required university degrees: Jürgen works in the marketing department of Radio Leipzig; Barbara is working for one of Germany's largest publishing firms; Jutta uses her language skills to not only teach, but also to translate English books into German.

Gerhard, as mentioned earlier, is a pensioner living in Berlin working with computers, and is "getting by," as he puts it.

CHAPTER NINETEEN

2014- 2015

In November 2014 Bonnie and I had the opportunity to meet all of our East German friends in Berlin. We extended a trip to France and Vienna just so we could be in Berlin for the twenty-fifth anniversary celebration marking the opening of the Wall. It was late in the evening of November 9, 1989 that the communist government made an announcement: All East Berliners – and in fact, all East Germans – could now travel to West Berlin without restrictions.

The Wall had opened and less than two years later a re-united Germany became a reality.

Our trip to Berlin gave us the opportunity, after so many years, to be with our friends. Gerhard, as noted earlier, still lives in Berlin; we were with him on two different days. Jürgen, Jutta and Barbara all came to Berlin from Leipzig, making it possible for us to share an entire day with them.

Let's start with Gerhard.

It's hard to believe that he and I had met each other in East Berlin over 40 years ago! He's the oldest of our four friends, and, as previously noted, retired.

My journal notes include the following: "Gerhard, 71 now, retired, pre-diabetic, shaved head, could lose weight. Rode his bike – no car. 'Much cheaper that way.' "

We met at a small outdoor café directly across from Tempelhof Airport. This was the only functioning major airport in West Berlin throughout the Cold War. It was therefore the landing site for the planes from the West during the Berlin Airlift of 1948-49. It's not in use now as an airport, having become a huge recreation area for the people of Berlin.

It was great seeing him again. There he sat, in that café, smiling and greeting my Bonnie and me with strong hugs.

After lots of talk about how things were going and his thanking us for bringing "California weather" to Berlin, we went across the street and onto the airfield of Tempelhof. We walked on the runways! Incredible: I never thought I would be able to do that, remembering its importance in the history of Berlin. I'd even landed there: My first trip to Berlin was in 1966, having flown from Frankfurt in a four-engine propeller-driven DC-6.

After an hour or so enjoying the open spaces of the airfield, it was back to the café for a cup of coffee. I finally asked him THE question: "What if the Wall were still standing – would you prefer that?"

He answered with a definite "yes." He told us that his life in the former East Germany was "secure," even without freedom. By "secure" he means that people had jobs, education, and health care. The cost of living was "affordable." "But now, people only care about money and are being exploited." The West is paying for what is still lacking in the East. And since he now lives in what was once West Berlin, he lives in "the West."

But he did admit, as I mentioned earlier, to having a "bit of rage" toward the GDR and its socialist system when he stood on the rim of the Grand Canyon some 20 years earlier.

It's not only the economic situation that irritates him. Immigration issues in Germany disturb him greatly:

> Immigrants– from Africa, the Middle East, the Roma [Gypsies]– are all over. They get a house or apartment from the government and in two weeks the place is a mess. They also contribute to our high crime rate.

Gerhard openly told us about his financial situation. His pension is a gross amount of 900 Euros per month. Here are his monthly expenses:

-200 Euros for taxes

-250 Euros for rent

-250 Euros left "to live on"

He told us he "just survives" and doesn't have any extra money to travel as he'd like. Part of the reason for that is that he "spent so much money on my two trips to the USA" in the early 1990s.

He'll never forget those trips; nor will he ever regret them.

He lives in a one-room apartment; he watches television a lot; he has three computers. He's handy at repairing computers, which brings in a little extra income each month. His life doesn't seem too exciting; he "loves to smoke and watch television."

It was clear to us, however, that he appreciates his freedom, even though reunification brought so many "negatives."

He also showed us some statistics that he'd written on a small piece of paper: In the last election, two of the states of East Germany that pushed the most for "freedom" in the late 1980s – Saxony and Brandenburg – participated least in the most recent election.

"You see – there are many other people who aren't happy with how things are going." It seems he feels that this lack of participation in elections is evidence that people just don't see much hope for the future. And when one combines that with the problems he says immigration has brought, Gerhard is extremely pessimistic about the future.

Yes – it is quite ironic he feels this way.

* * *

Wednesday, November 5, 2014 was a great day, for we saw our friends from Leipzig. Jürgen, Barbara, Jutta, and her husband Matheus, all came to Berlin. We had made arrangements to see them during the week of the celebrations marking the 25th anniversary of the fall of the Wall.

It was an incredible day: 31 years after meeting them in Leipzig, we were in Berlin together. Lots of hugs, laughs, and, of course, reminiscing: Barbara meeting Ivan and me at the train station as we arrived for our German teachers' seminar in Leipzig in the summer of 1983; times together in Leipzig as we became friends; the Beatles' "Let It Be" playing on Jutta's stereo in her apartment when I asked her if she ever thought she'd be able to travel to California; being together in Berlin in December, 1989, for the opening of the Brandenburg Gate; Ivan's and my enjoying the Christmas goose with Jürgen and Barbara in her apartment after the Gate opened; Jürgen's and Jutta's visits to us in California in the 1990s; and, of course, so many letters exchanged over three decades.

And how are they doing in November of 2014? Quite well, actually.

Jutta, as we've already learned, is still teaching, writing, translating and traveling extensively; this is in addition to "trying to stay fit by doing my favorite physical activities: inline skating and aqua jogging." She has no car (Matheus does) and "I don't want or need one."

Barbara still works for the firm that publishes school texts. I asked her about memories of the Wall from the 1980s. She remembers one time when she was in East Berlin. There was a carnival in West Berlin with a Ferris wheel; from the East she could hear music and screams of excitement from the people riding it. And thinking: "The Wall will *never* come down in my lifetime."

Jürgen is still working at Radio Leipzig in the marketing department. "But now we're number two." He's settled into his career working there and still travels a lot: As I write this, (February, 2015) he's in South Africa.

So – three out of the four are very happy with their lives in a democratic and capitalist Germany. They admit to having believed it would never happen. But it did. There is definitely, for the Leipzigers, no longing for the "old days."

The exception, as we've learned, is Gerhard in Berlin. He admits to believing his situation would be better if there still were the German Democratic Republic. In February 2015, he wrote to me in an email that he sincerely believes the "flood" of Muslim immigrants is destroying Germany; the German government, because of its inaction to counteract this, is leading Germany down a disastrous path. The health-care system is being destroyed; German doctors are fleeing to Scandinavia and Switzerland; 25% of German workers live on (what Gerhard considers) poverty wages.

* * *

I'd like to add here some personal reflection and memories of this most recent time in Berlin, November 1-11, 2014:

Our days prior to the celebrations on November 9 were

active and rewarding: We bicycled through Berlin's "Central Park," the *Tiergarten*, on a crisp fall day, enjoying the scenic gardens with fall colors; we spent several hours in the beautiful residential district of Grunewald; we shopped and had dinner in KaDeWe, Berlin's premier department store; we attended a Bach cantata in Kaiser Wilhelm Memorial Church. And we visited, with Gerhard, some place we had never been: the "Gardens of the World" located in the Berlin suburb of Marzahn, which still has that "GDR look" of socialist apartment blocks.

And, of course, we went to Checkpoint Charlie, the American-manned border crossing into East Berlin from 1948 until 1990. Today it's a rather large tourist attraction, but still very worth experiencing, with "American" and "Russian" soldiers dressed in their military uniforms. They're happy to have their picture taken with you – for a tip, of course.

If West and East Berlin still existed, it goes without saying not all of this would be possible today, which leads me to include here some personal observations of the city today:

Berlin never lets one forget its history and the history of Germany. We spent several hours in the German History Museum where there are superb expositions of not only "old Germany," but also a very complete and honest presentation of the National Socialist years and the Holocaust.

A constant theme throughout Germany is *nie wieder*, or "never again," when referring to the Holocaust. Berlin does not let one forget: The names of all the death camps are on a permanent memorial sign outside of the Wittenbergplatz subway station in the center of Berlin. The sites of these camps can be visited today and are memorials to the atrocities of the Holocaust.

Very close to the Brandenburg Gate is the "Memorial to the Murdered Jews of Europe," an area of nearly five acres made up of stone blocks of various sizes. When one walks through the memorial, one gets the feeling of being lost in some type of maze. It's designed to be symbolic of the mental experience the Jews of Germany must have experienced during the Holocaust.

The German History Museum also has an excellent section on the events leading up to *Die Wende*. It thoroughly covers the months before the fall of the Wall, beginning with the church services in the Nikolai Church and the Monday demonstrations in Leipzig, concluding with the events in Berlin leading up to the announcement that citizens of the German Democratic Republic were free to travel to West Berlin without special permission.

One of the most memorable displays in the museum is a collection of hand-painted signs done by children. They are copies of signs and banners the East Germans used in the demonstrations leading up to *Die Wende*. Here are some examples:

Wir sind das Volk – We are the People!
Wende statt Wände – Change Instead of Walls!

Die Gedanken sind Frei! – Thoughts Are Free!

Wir brauchen Hoffnung – We need hope!

We also visited the Reichstag. The view from the top of Germany's Parliament building at night is incredible. From the roof of the most important historical building in Berlin, we could see the *Lichtergrenze*, or "Border of Lights": 8,000 lighted and helium-filled balloons set up to trace the nine-mile long path of the Wall through central Berlin. (Balloons were used to remind one of the thousands of candles people carried during the peaceful demonstrations of 1989.) Each balloon also had a "patron," who, on November 9, 2014, at 10:00 PM released his or her balloon with a personal message regarding the anniversary.

Here are a few examples of these messages, which I've translated from German, taken from material handed out during the celebration:

- I've come with my dad and am already so curious.
- 25 years of the fall of the Wall prove: Peace is attained through words, not weapons.
- I hope the history of this city will never be forgotten, so that we will always understand it and learn from it. Berlin is for me a living book of history.

The balloons' release took place during the playing of Beethoven's Ninth Symphony by the Berlin philharmonic. This was the highlight of the evening that we experienced at the

Brandenburg Gate on the evening of November 9, 2014. We stood but 100 feet from the stage that had been erected on the west side of the Gate. Choirs sang, dancers danced, speeches commemorating *Die Wende* were given; those who died trying to escape East Berlin were again recognized. Also singing was Wolf Biermann, the dissident East German folk singer who, in 1964, was not permitted by the communist government to return to East Germany after a West German performance.

Mikhail Gorbachev, a person I never thought I'd ever see in person, also appeared on that stage. As Secretary General of the Soviet Union in the 1980s it was "Gorby's" policies of *perestroika* and *glasnost* that convinced the East Germans that the Soviets would not put down their peaceful revolution. Gorbachev in effect told the East German government: "Let happen what's going to happen."

Die Wende took place.

Many Germans today consider Mr. Gorbachev a hero.

Also on the stage was another important historical person: Lech Walesa, leader of the Solidarity labor movement in Poland in the 1980s. Solidarity became what amounted to be the first independent trade union in the Soviet Bloc, leading to the eventual collapse of the Communist regime in Poland.

Mr. Walesa became a significant inspiration to those in East Germany who also found themselves on the path to more freedom.

The Soviet empire began to crumble because of these two individuals. And they were in Berlin on November 9, 2014.

Fireworks and rock music concluded an unforgettable evening. My final journal entry: "We stood for more than two hours, but it was well worth it. These people have been through a lot – and only want the best for the rest of the world – for all peoples."

* * *

Email correspondence with our friends continues after those memorable days in Berlin. We all exchanged Christmas greetings, with Jürgen writing:

> The day together in Berlin was a great experience for me, too. I'm always thinking about it. It makes us so happy that you're still interested in us!! Thank you so very much for the great day!

* * *

Gerhard, however, took a very different tone in his Christmas email, after I had written about how much we enjoyed being with him in Berlin.

> I'm sorry that I can't share your enthusiasm about the fall of the Wall. For all my acquaintances and me it only brought disadvantages.
>
> When I was able to get to West Berlin in August of 1989, I left behind a fully furnished two-room apartment, a Trabant [East

Germany's ubiquitous automobile], a motorcycle, and the East Mark, which went a long way.

I couldn't tell my brother or sister anything about this beforehand – they were members of the Communist Party.

In West Berlin I received 100 West Marks, lodging in a container, and had to see how things would work out. I knew that through hard work I could reach a much higher standard of living.

He then writes reality soon set in. 17 million East Germans received the 100 Marks of "welcome money". That came to 1.7 *billion* Marks, which simply was not affordable, in his opinion. "And who knows how many more billions disappeared in the East?" he asks. In Gerhard's opinion, the price for this was drastically diminished social services and reduced pensions for all *Wessis*. He continues by writing that the Federal Republic (West Germany) was a strong, socially responsible country. But rising debt and shortages are causing huge problems. This is compounded by immigration from Muslim countries, Eastern Europe, and Africa, which is leading to increased opposition throughout Germany to German Prime Minister Angela Merkel's policies.

Gerhard also mentions a resurgence of anti-immigrant movements. The most vociferous is PEGIDA, or *Patriotische Europäer gegen die Islamisierung des Abendlands*, which in English translates as: "Patriotic Europeans Against the Islamization of the West." "Immigrants out, go back to where you came from" seems to be their message.

He concludes with a comment on Germany's political leadership: "[Chancellor] Merkel doesn't have a clue. I can't wait for the next election. Please forgive me for all the bitterness I have."

How can I not? I understand what he's saying. It makes me sad he feels this way. I believe most Germans would not agree with him; my other East German friends certainly don't seem to, for they are living comfortably, have good professional level careers, travel extensively, and seem very pleased with a united Germany. But they are not retired and living on a pension that is mainly funded by decades of working in communist East Germany.

David F. Strack

CHAPTER TWENTY
Zum Schluss – In Conclusion

It's mid-April 2015 as I write this, nearly forty-one years since that "beautiful sunny July afternoon in East Berlin" when we met Gerhard; nine years later, we were fortunate enough to meet Jürgen, Barbara, and Jutta in Leipzig. True friendships developed between these East Germans and our small group of American teachers of German, and they continue today.

It's now time to conclude this chronicle.

Maybe our four friends represent how all Germans feel today about their situation. I have no statistics to back this up, but I think it's at least an interesting thought: 75% - Jürgen, Barbara, and Jutta - are satisfied and happy with what has happened in Germany since *Die Wende*; 25% - Gerhard – is not happy with the present situation in Germany, but he is free and treasures his two trips to America.

(Oh, wait! I **do** have statistics to back this up! I just looked up a Gallup Poll taken in 2014 – their "Positive Experience Index" has 77% of Germans responding positively. So, maybe my East German friends are quite representative of the way Germans in general feel about how their lives are going. Interesting.)

With freedom comes travel, and if travel is an indication of living life to its fullest, Jutta is a classic example: she and her husband Michael are in Tibet as I write this, having also cruised the Yangtze River in China.

Jürgen has also been traveling. He's just returned from South Africa, where he and his friends enjoyed a safari vacation. He writes in his most recent email that they gave their trip a title, so to speak: "South Africa Enjoyed Through All the Senses." Their group even stayed at a lodge run by Germans from Saxony, which is in the former East Germany. The safaris they took included: "antelope, landscape, 'big five' [whatever that is], and river."

> And we experienced in their natural environments giraffes, water buffaloes, cheetahs, rhinos, a leopard, and hippos. It's unbelievable how beautiful these animals are! [The photos he sent me per email verify this.]

How the lives of my friends have changed: Jürgen wrote in 1989 that he thought the Wall would never come down. It did — and now he's in the marketing department of Radio Leipzig and enjoying safaris in Africa; Jutta is a university professor in Leipzig and able to travel extensively; Barbara has her doctorate, a career at a well-known publishing house, and a sixteen-year-old daughter who wants to come to the USA; Gerhard, while so very critical of Germany today, values his freedom and will never forget his two journeys to America.

Thank Goodness for *Die Wende* and those who were brave enough to take East Germany down that path.

I am so thankful that I met them and we became friends. Knowing them and knowing what they've been through has helped me appreciate the freedom I have had my entire life and for which I have never had to struggle. I think back on our departures at the "Palace of Tears" in East Berlin — so aptly named because of the tears that were shed there when we could go back into West Berlin, and our friends had to stay in East Berlin and continue their restricted lives in a socialist country.

My friends and I still communicate regularly, and not only through email. Jutta's Christmas letter to friends and family of 2014 actually came via air-mail and quoting from it is, I believe, an appropriate place to conclude this chronicle. Most of the letter is a summary of her family's year: travel, problems, anniversaries, her kids' activities and accomplishments, studies in Great Britain, and her translation work.

Here is her concluding paragraph, which I find so appropriate in the context of what I'm trying to communicate with these letters from East Germany:

> In early November Michael and I went to Berlin so we could meet with our friends Bonnie and David. I got to know David at the Herder Institute [Karl Marx University] German teachers' summer seminar during those dark times in 1983.

He's always written to me, holding my hopes high that we would see each other again, always assuring me that someday the GDR would be behind me and I would be free. In 1998 the boys and I visited him in California, and he and Bonnie have been in Leipzig to visit us. And in Berlin we were able to happily celebrate together the fall of the Wall. It's just incomprehensible that 25 years ago the prison opened, and the storm of freedom blew over us. May this storm always pull us to a spirit of insubordination and confrontation, and keep us active and never let us forget that we must constantly defend this freedom and plurality, with which we have now grown up, against ignorance and ideologues of all kinds, as we always look to the future.

Jutta ends her letter with a quote, in German, from George Washington. It summarizes so well something I've learned through these forty years of friendship and correspondence with my East German friends:

Die Freiheit, hat sie erst einmal Wurzeln geschlagen, ist eine schnell wachsende Pflanze.

Liberty, when it begins to take root, is a plant of rapid growth.

About the Author
David F. Strack

For over 45 years, David F. Strack taught German at both the high school and college level, finishing his career as an adjunct professor of German at the University of Redlands. He received his Bachelor of Arts degree in history and German from the University of Redlands and his Master's degree in German from Middlebury College.

As part of his love of the language and culture, David traveled extensively in Europe, including several times to East Germany, the German Democratic Republic. There he became friends with four individuals who were striving to live normal lives in the communist state. For decades these friends exchanged letters with David, sharing their dreams and frustrations. His first book, LETTERS OVER THE WALL, brings you into the personal lives of everyday East Germans.

In addition to leading many student and adult tour groups to Germany and Austria, David also taught English in Germany as a Fulbright Exchange Teacher. He is now retired from teaching and is living in Yucaipa, California. He still corresponds with his friends in Germany, and visits them whenever possible.

Printed in Great Britain
by Amazon